A PERSONAL ANTHOLOGY

Also by Jorge Luis Borges
Published by Grove Press

Ficciones

Jorge Luis Borges

A PERSONAL ANTHOLOGY

Edited and with a Foreword by Anthony Kerrigan

GROVE PRESS, INC. / NEW YORK

Originally published as *Antología Personal,* © 1961 by Editorial
Sur, S.A., Buenos Aires.

First Evergreen Edition 1968
Twelfth Printing 1982
ISBN: 0-394-17270-1
Library of Congress Catalog Card Number: 67-29764

Manufactured in the United States of America

GROVE PRESS, INC., 196 West Houston Street,
New York, N.Y. 10014

CONTENTS

FOREWORD

Jorge Luis Borges is most poignantly and hauntingly interested in what men have believed in their doubt: Siddhartha, Josaphat, the Face of Christ; Duns Scotus, Averröes, Berkeley, Hume; Judaism, its offshoot Christianity, Buddhism, Hinduism, Idealism. His equivocation regarding heresies and dogmas renews them all, though he may be the unique evocative source of his own nostalgic non-belief in Belief or prescient belief in non-belief.

A fundamental theme always close to hand is his own identity. Like Don Quixote, he does not mind being a character in a book, so long as it is in the *right* book and not the *wrong* one. Don Quixote objected, in the *Second Part of Don Quixote*, by Cervantes, to appearing in the (spurious) *Second Part of Don Quixote*, by Avellaneda; Borges puts the question: "Is not *one single term repeated* enough to break down and confound the history of the world?" The right book for him to appear in, then, is the one by "Borges." And no other. As for the present, he merely identifies himself as the "one who swears he has not died."

(The identity of others concerned in the present book is dimly asseverated by their names at the end of each piece they translated. They are Americans and a Scotsman who have put into American and into English some of the thoughts Borges has had in various languages—even in English—before he wrote them down in Spanish.)

Borges' concern with "history" is unique. He is not taken with the grandiose Goethean-Romantic pivotal zeniths of Spenglerian cycles, or even with Unamuno's "intra-history" of dim daily existential Everyman routine, as he is moved by the epiphanies of racial and folk evolution. In the story of *The Warrior and the Captive,* he intuits a barbarian warrior's physic conversion to Rome as a city of light and order, and, conversely, of the Englishwoman's atavistic return to savagery in the vastness of the Argentine waste. Men leave off being wild beasts in one divine moment, or return to the earth to drink the blood of a slaughtered animal in another moment equally divine; enemies become blood brothers in the heat of battle, or a pursuer joins the prey in a paroxysm of blood identification (*Biography of Tadeo Isidoro Cruz*).

And as for History's periods, those Grand Ages of a Hero or of a God, they die out, period by period, in the physical death of a last survivor (as in *The Witness*), and the world is the "poorer."

History is also the epiphany of epigram: *six feet of English earth for Harald Sigurdson; the odor of horses and of courage; I was proud of the men who had killed my brothers*: these are the elements of what Borges calls "true history," the vocabulary of *The Modesty of History*.

Among his several obsessions, Borges has counted a knife, The Knife. He is "animated" by the feel of it, he fictionally clutches it on behalf of others, he is atrociously aware of it, altogether frustrated, lying, unfulfilled, in his desk drawer, among his rough drafts and letters. A knife, moreover, the knife in his thoughts, is to kill; it was "conceived and given form for a very special purpose." In addition, there is, in his verse, "An impossible recollection of having died/Fighting, on some corner of a suburb." The Knife in his drawer should perforce fulfill its destiny; otherwise "so much hard faith, such impassively innocent arrogance" is rendered vain by non-use. An obsession with dying is proof of being alive; an obsession with a manner of dying, with being killed or killing, even more, is a creatively morbid concern with the diabolic importance of (someone's) being alive. This compulsive instinct is, perhaps, a true measure of Borges: it leads him to think, to assert, that if in the universe—in the entire history of the universe even—there is or has ever been anyone who could be a duplicate of himself, then the meaning of all life, all lives, is altogether suspect.

The present collection is the attestation that no one is, ever has been, his replica. There is "Borges and I," Borges and The Other, but there is, on the present evidence, no other Borges.

—Anthony Kerrigan

Dublin, 1967

All the pieces presented here in English are complete versions of their originals in Spanish.

PROLOGUE

My preferences have dictated this book. I should like to be
judged by it, justified or reproved because of it, and not by
certain exercises in excessive and apocryphal local color
which keep cropping up in anthologies and which I can not
recall without a blush. To a chronological order I have preferred one of "sympathies and differences." I have thereby
proved, once again, my fundamental paucity: *The Circular
Ruins*, which dates from 1939, prefigures *The Golem* or
Chess, which are practically of the present. This paucity
does not dishearten me, since it provides an illusion of continuity.

Croce held that art is expression; to this exigency, or to
a deformation of this exigency, we owe the worst literature
of our time. True enough, Paul Valéry was able to write with
felicity:

> *Comme le fruit se fond en puissance,*
> *Comme en délice il change son absence*
> *Dans une bouche où sa forme se meurt*

and Tennyson could write:

> *. . . . . .and saw,*
> *Straining his eyes beneath an arch of hand,*
> *Or thought he saw, the speck that bore the King,*
> *Down that long water opening on the deep*
> *Somewhere far off, pass on and on, and go*
> *From less to less and vanish into light.*

verses which reproduce a mental process with precision; but
such victories are rare and no one (I believe) will judge
them the most lasting or necessary words in literature. Some-

times, I, too, sought expression. I know now that my gods grant me no more than allusion or mention.

Buenos Aires
August 16, 1961

—J.L.B.

A PERSONAL ANTHOLOGY

DEATH AND THE COMPASS

Of the many problems which exercised the daring perspicacity of Lönnrot none was so strange—so harshly strange, we may say—as the staggered series of bloody acts which culminated at the villa of Triste-le-Roy, amid the boundless odor of the eucalypti. It is true that Erik Lönnrot did not succeed in preventing the last crime, but it is indisputable that he foresaw it. Nor did he, of course, guess the identity of Yarmolinsky's unfortunate assassin, but he did divine the secret morphology of the vicious series as well as the participation of Red Scharlach, whose alias is Scharlach the Dandy. This criminal (as so many others) had sworn on his honor to kill Lönnrot, but the latter had never allowed himself to be intimidated. Lönnrot thought of himself as a pure thinker, an Auguste Dupin, but there was something of the adventurer in him, and even of the gamester.

The first crime occurred at the Hôtel du Nord—that high prism that dominates the estuary whose waters are the colors of the desert. To this tower (which most manifestly unites the hateful whiteness of a sanitarium, the numbered divisibility of a prison, and the general appearance of a bawdy house) on the third day of December came the delegate from Podolsk to the Third Talmudic Congress, Doctor Marcel Yarmolinsky, a man of gray beard and gray eyes. We shall never know whether the Hôtel du Nord pleased him: he accepted it with the ancient resignation which had allowed him to endure three years of war in the Carpathians and three thousand years of oppression and pogroms. He was given a sleeping room on floor R, in front of the suite which the Tetrarch of Galilee occupied not without some splendor. Yarmolinsky supped, postponed until the following day an investigation of the unknown city, arranged upon a cupboard

1

his many books and his few possessions, and before midnight turned off the light. (Thus declared the Tetrarch's chauffeur, who slept in an adjoining room.) On the fourth, at 11:03 A.M., there was a telephone call for him from the editor of the *Yiddische Zeitung*; Doctor Yarmolinsky did not reply; he was found in his room, his face already a little dark, and his body, almost nude, beneath a large anachronistic cape. He was lying not far from the door which gave onto the corridor; a deep stab wound had split open his breast. In the same room, a couple of hours later, in the midst of journalists, photographers, and police, Commissioner Treviranus and Lönnrot were discussing the problem with equanimity.

"There's no need to look for a Chimera, or a cat with three legs," Treviranus was saying as he brandished an imperious cigar. "We all know that the Tetrarch of Galilee is the possessor of the finest sapphires in the world. Someone, intending to steal them, came in here by mistake. Yarmolinsky got up; the robber had to kill him. What do you think?"

"It's possible, but not interesting," Lönnrot answered. "You will reply that reality hasn't the slightest need to be of interest. And I'll answer you that reality may avoid the obligation to be interesting, but that hypotheses may not. In the hypothesis you have postulated, chance intervenes largely. Here lies a dead rabbi; I should prefer a purely rabbinical explanation; not the imaginary mischances of an imaginary robber."

Treviranus answered ill-humoredly:

"I am not interested in rabbinical explanations; I am interested in the capture of the man who stabbed this unknown person."

"Not so unknown," corrected Lönnrot. "Here are his complete works." He indicated a line of tall volumes: *A Vindication of the Cabala; An Examination of the Philosophy of Robert Fludd;* a literal translation of the *Sepher Yezirah;* a *Biography of the Baal Shem;* a *History of the Sect of the Hasidim;* a monograph (in German) on the Tetragrammaton; another, on the divine nomenclature of the Pentateuch. The Commissioner gazed at them with suspicion, almost with revulsion. Then he fell to laughing.

"I'm only a poor Christian," he replied. "Carry off all these moth-eaten classics if you like; I haven't got time to lose in Jewish superstitions."

"Maybe this crime belongs to the history of Jewish superstitions," murmured Lönnrot.

"Like Christianity," the editor of the *Yiddische Zeitung* dared to put in. He was a myope, an atheist, and very timid.

No one answered him. One of the agents had found inserted in the small typewriter a piece of paper on which was written the following inconclusive sentence.

The first letter of the Name has been spoken

Lönnrot abstained from smiling. Suddenly become a bibliophile—or Hebraist—he directed that the dead man's books be made into a parcel, and he carried them to his office. Indifferent to the police investigation, he dedicated himself to studying them. A large octavo volume revealed to him the teachings of Israel Baal Shem-Tob, founder of the sect of the Pious; another volume, the virtues and terrors of the Tetragrammaton, which is the ineffable name of God; another, the thesis that God has a secret name, in which is epitomized (as in the crystal sphere which the Persians attribute to Alexander of Macedon) his ninth attribute, eternity—that is to say, the immediate knowledge of everything that will exist, exists, and has existed in the universe. Tradition numbers ninety-nine names of God; the Hebraists attribute this imperfect number to the magical fear of even numbers; the Hasidim reason that this hiatus indicates a hundredth name—the Absolute Name.

From this erudition he was distracted, within a few days, by the appearance of the editor of the *Yiddische Zeitung*. This man wished to talk of the assassination; Lönnrot preferred to speak of the diverse names of God. The journalist declared, in three columns, that the investigator Erik Lönnrot had dedicated himself to studying the names of God in order to "come up with" the name of the assassin. Lönnrot, habituated to the simplifications of journalism, did not become indignant. One of those shopkeepers who have found that there are buyers for every book came out with a popular edition of the *History of the Sect of the Hasidim*.

The second crime occurred on the night of the third of January, in the most deserted and empty corner of the capital's western suburbs. Toward dawn, one of the gendarmes who patrol these lonely places on horseback detected a man in a cape, lying prone in the shadow of an ancient paint shop. The hard visage seemed bathed in blood; a deep stab wound had split open his breast. On the wall, upon the yellow and red rhombs, there were some words written in chalk. The gendarme spelled them out. . . .

That afternoon Treviranus and Lönnrot made their way toward the remote scene of the crime. To the left and right of the automobile, the city disintegrated; the firmament grew larger and the houses meant less and less and a brick kiln or a poplar grove more and more. They reached their miserable destination: a final alley of rose-colored mud walls which in some way seemed to reflect the disordered setting of the sun. The dead man had already been identified. He was Daniel Simon Azevedo, a man of some fame in the ancient northern suburbs, who had risen from wagoner to political tough, only to degenerate later into a thief and even an informer. (The singular style of his death struck them as appropriate: Azevedo was the last representative of a generation of bandits who knew how to handle a dagger, but not a revolver.) The words in chalk were the following:

The second letter of the Name has been spoken

The third crime occurred on the night of the third of February. A little before one o'clock, the telephone rang in the office of Commissioner Treviranus. In avid secretiveness a man with a guttural voice spoke: he said his name was Ginzberg (or Ginsburg) and that he was disposed to communicate, for a reasonable remuneration, an explanation of the two sacrifices of Azevedo and Yarmolinsky. The discordant sound of whistles and horns drowned out the voice of the informer. Then the connection was cut off. Without rejecting the possibility of a hoax (it was carnival time), Treviranus checked and found he had been called from Liverpool House, a tavern on the Rue de Toulon—that dirty street where cheek by jowl are the peepshow and the milk store, the bordello and the women selling Bibles. Treviranus called back and spoke to the owner. This personage (Black Finnegan by name, an old Irish criminal who was crushed, annihilated almost, by respectability) told him that the last person to use the establishment's phone had been a lodger, a certain Gryphius, who had just gone out with some friends. Treviranus immediately went to Liverpool House where Finnegan related the following facts. Eight days previously, Gryphius had taken a room above the saloon. He was a man of sharp features, a nebulous gray beard, shabbily clothed in black; Finnegan (who put the room to a use which Treviranus guessed) demanded a rent which was undoubtedly excessive; Gryphius immediately paid the stipulated sum. He scarcely ever went out; he dined and lunched in his room; his face was hardly known in the bar. On this particular night, he came down to telephone from Finnegan's office. A closed coupe stopped in front of the tavern. The driver did not move from his seat; several of the patrons recalled that he was wearing a bear mask. Two harlequins descended from the coupe; they were short in stature, and no one could fail to observe that they were very drunk. With a tooting of horns they burst into Finnegan's office; they embraced Gryphius, who seemed to recognize them but who replied to them coldly; they exchanged a few words in Yiddish—he, in a low guttural voice; they, in shrill, falsetto tones—and then the party climbed to the upstairs room. Within a quarter hour the three descended, very joyous; Gryphius, staggering, seemed as drunk as the others. He walked—tall, dazed—in the middle, between the masked harlequins. (One of the women in the bar remembered the yellow, red and green rhombs, the diamond designs.) Twice he stumbled; twice he was held up by the harlequins. Alongside the adjoining dock basin, whose water was rectangular, the trio got into the coupe and disappeared. From the running board, the last of the harlequins had scrawled an obscene figure and a sentence on one of the slates of the outdoor shed.

Treviranus gazed upon the sentence. It was nearly foreknowable. It read:

The last of the letters of the Name has been spoken

He examined, then, the small room of Gryphius-Ginzberg. On the floor was a violent star of blood; in the corners, the remains of some Hungarian-brand cigarettes; in a cabinet, a book in Latin—the *Philologus Hebraeo-Graecus* (1739) of Leusden—along with various manuscript notes. Treviranus studied the book with indignation and had Lönnrot summoned. The latter, without taking off his hat, began to read while the Commissioner questioned the contradictory witnesses to the possible kidnaping. At four in the morning they came out. In the tortuous Rue de Toulon, as they stepped on the dead serpentines of the dawn, Treviranus said:

"And supposing the story of this night were a sham?"

Erik Lönnrot smiled and read him with due gravity a

passage (underlined) of the thirty-third dissertation of the *Philologus:*

> *Dies Judaeorum incipit a solis occasu*
> *usque ad solis occasum diei sequentis.*

"This means," he added, "that *the Hebrew day begins at sundown and lasts until the following sundown.*"

Treviranus attempted an irony.

"Is this fact the most worthwhile you've picked up to-night?"

"No. Of even greater value is a word Ginzberg used."

The afternoon dailies did not neglect this series of disappearances. *The Cross and the Sword* contrasted them with the admirable discipline and order of the last Eremitical Congress; Ernest Palast, writing in *The Martyr,* spoke out against "the intolerable delays in this clandestine and frugal pogrom, which has taken three months to liquidate three Jews"; the *Yiddische Zeitung* rejected the terrible hypothesis of an anti-Semitic plot, "even though many discerning intellects do not admit of any other solution to the triple mystery"; the most illustrious gunman in the South, Dandy Red Scharlach, swore that in his district such crimes as these would never occur, and he accused Commissioner Franz Treviranus of criminal negligence.

On the night of March first, the Commissioner received an imposing-looking, sealed envelope. He opened it: the envelope contained a letter signed Baruj Spinoza, and a detailed plan of the city, obviously torn from a Baedeker. The letter prophesied that on the third of March there would *not* be a fourth crime, inasmuch as the paint shop in the West, the Tavern on the Rue de Toulon and the Hôtel du Nord were the "perfect vertices of an equilateral and mystic triangle"; the regularity of this triangle was made clear on the map with red ink. This argument, *more geometrico,* Treviranus read with resignation, and sent the letter and map on to Lönnrot—who deserved such a piece of insanity.

Erik Lönnrot studied the documents. The three sites were in fact equidistant. Symmetry in time (the third of December, the third of January, the third of February); symmetry in space as well. . . . Of a sudden he sensed he was about to decipher the mystery. A set of calipers and a compass completed his sudden intuition. He smiled, pronounced the word "Tetragrammaton" (of recent acquisition), and called the Commissioner on the telephone. He told him:

"Thank you for the equilateral triangle you sent me last night. It has enabled me to solve the problem. Tomorrow, Friday, the criminals will be in jail, we can rest assured."

"In that case, they're not planning a fourth crime?"

"Precisely because they *are* planning a fourth crime can we rest assured."

Lönnrot hung up. An hour later he was traveling in one of the trains of the Southern Railways, en route to the abandoned villa of Triste-le-Roy. South of the city of our story there flows a blind little river filled with muddy water made disgraceful by floating scraps and garbage. On the further side is a manufacturing suburb where, under the protection of a chief from Barcelona, gunmen flourish. Lönnrot smiled to himself to think that the most famous of them— Red Scharlach—would have given anything to know of this clandestine visit. Azevedo had been a comrade of Scharlach's; Lönnrot considered the remote possibility that the fourth victim might be Scharlach himself. Then, he put aside the thought. . . . He had virtually deciphered the problem; the mere circumstances, or the reality (names, prison records, faces, judicial and penal proceedings), scarcely interested him now. Most of all he wanted to take a stroll, to relax from three months of sedentary investigation. He reflected on how the explanation of the crimes lay in an anonymous triangle and a dust-laden Greek word. The mystery seemed to him almost crystalline now; he was mortified to have dedicated a hundred days to it.

The train stopped at a silent loading platform. Lönnrot descended. It was one of those deserted afternoons which seem like dawn. The air over the muddy plain was damp and cold. Lönnrot set off across the fields. He saw dogs, he saw a wagon on a dead road, he saw the horizon, he saw a silvery horse drinking the crapulous water of a puddle. Dusk was falling when he saw the rectangular belvedere of the villa of Triste-le-Roy, almost as tall as the black eucalypti which surrounded it. He thought of the fact that only one more dawn and one more nightfall (an ancient splendor in the east, and another in the west) separated him from the hour so much desired by the seekers of the Name.

A rust-colored wrought-iron fence defined the irregular perimeter of the villa. The main gate was closed. Without much expectation of entering, Lönnrot made a complete circuit. In front of the insurmountable gate once again, he put his hand between the bars almost mechanically and chanced upon the bolt. The creaking of the iron surprised him. With laborious passivity the entire gate gave way.

Lönnrot advanced among the eucalypti, stepping amidst confused generations of rigid, broken leaves. Close up, the house on the estate of Triste-le-Roy was seen to abound in superfluous symmetries and in maniacal repetitions: a glacial Diana in one lugubrious niche was complemented by another Diana in another niche; one balcony was repeated by another balcony; double steps of stairs opened into a double balustrade. A two-faced Hermes cast a monstrous shadow. Lönnrot circled the house as he had the estate. He examined everything; beneath the level of the terrace he noticed a narrow shutter door.

He pushed against it: some marble steps descended to a vault. Versed now in the architect's preferences, Lönnrot divined that there would be a set of stairs on the opposite wall. He found them, ascended, raised his hands, and pushed up a trap door.

The diffusion of light guided him to a window. He opened it: a round, yellow moon outlined two stopped-up fountains in the melancholy garden. Lönnrot explored the house. He traveled through antechambers and galleries to emerge upon duplicate patios; several times he emerged upon the same patio. He ascended dust-covered stairways and came out into circular antechambers; he was infinitely reflected in opposing mirrors; he grew weary of opening or half-opening windows which revealed the same desolate garden outside, from various heights and various angles; inside, the furniture was wrapped in yellow covers and the chandeliers bound up with cretonne. A bedroom detained him; in the bedroom, a single rose in a porcelain vase—at the first touch the ancient petals fell apart. On the second floor, on the top story, the house seemed to be infinite and growing. *The house is not this large,* he thought. *It is only made larger by the penumbra, the symmetry, the mirrors, the years, my ignorance, the solitude.*

Going up a spiral staircase he arrived at the observatory. The evening moon shone through the rhomboid diamonds of the windows, which were yellow, red and green. He was brought to a halt by a stunning and dizzying recollection.

Two men of short stature, ferocious and stocky, hurled themselves upon him and took his weapon. Another man, very tall, saluted him gravely, and said:

"You are very thoughtful. You've saved us a night and a day."

It was Red Scharlach. His men manacled Lönnrot's hands. Lönnrot at length found his voice.

"Are you looking for the Secret Name, Scharlach?"

Scharlach remained standing, indifferent. He had not participated in the short struggle; he scarcely stretched out his hand to receive Lönnrot's revolver. He spoke; in his voice

Lönnrot detected a fatigued triumph, a hatred the size of the universe, a sadness no smaller than that hatred.

"No," answered Scharlach. "I am looking for something more ephemeral and slippery, I am looking for Erik Lönnrot. Three years ago, in a gambling house on the Rue de Toulon, you arrested my brother and had him sent to prison. In the exchange of shots that night my men got me away in a coupe, with a police bullet in my chest. Nine days and nine nights I lay dying in this desolate, symmetrical villa; I was racked with fever, and the odious double-faced Janus who gazes toward the twilights of dusk and dawn terrorized my dreams and my waking. I learned to abominate my body, I came to feel that two eyes, two hands, two lungs are as monstrous as two faces. An Irishman attempted to convert me to the faith of Jesus; he repeated to me that famous axiom of the *goyim:* All roads lead to Rome. At night, my delirium nurtured itself on this metaphor: I sensed that the world was a labyrinth, from which it was impossible to flee, for all paths, whether they seemed to lead north or south, actually led to Rome, which was also the quadrilateral jail where my brother was dying and the villa of Triste-le-Roy. During those nights I swore by the god who sees from two faces, and by all the gods of fever and of mirrors, to weave a labyrinth around the man who had imprisoned my brother. I have woven it, and it holds: the materials are a dead writer on heresies, a compass, an eighteenth-century sect, a Greek word, a dagger, the rhombs of a paint shop.

"The first objective in the sequence was given me by chance. I had made plans with some colleagues—among them, Daniel Azevedo—to take the Tetrarch's sapphires. Azevedo betrayed us; with the money we advanced him he got himself inebriated and started on the job a day early. In the vastness of the hotel he got lost; at two in the morning he blundered into Yarmolinsky's room. The latter, harassed by insomnia, had set himself to writing. He was editing some notes, apparently, or writing an article on the Name of God; he had just written the words *The first letter of the Name has been spoken*. Azevedo enjoined him to be quiet; Yarmolinsky reached out his hand for the bell which would arouse all the hotel's forces; Azevedo at once stabbed him in the chest. It was almost a reflex action: half a century of violence had taught him that it was easiest and surest to kill. . . . Ten days later, I learned through the *Yiddische Zeitung* that you were perusing the writings of Yarmolinsky for the key to his death. For my part I read the *History of the Sect of the Hasidim;* I learned that the reverent fear of pronouncing the Name of God had given rise to the doctrine that this Name is all-powerful and mystic. I learned that some Hasidim, in search of this secret Name, had gone as far as to offer human sacrifices. . . . I knew you would conjecture that the Hasidim had sacrificed the rabbi; I set myself to justifying this conjecture.

"Marcel Yarmolinsky died on the night of December third; for the second sacrifice I selected the night of January third. Yarmolinsky died in the North; for the second sacrifice a place in the West was preferable. Daniel Azevedo was the inevitable victim. He deserved death: he was an impulsive person, a traitor; his capture could destroy the entire plan. One of our men stabbed him; in order to link his corpse to the other one I wrote on the paint shop diamonds *The second letter of the Name has been spoken*.

"The third 'crime' was produced on the third of February. It was as Treviranus must have guessed, a mere mockery, a simulacrum. I am Gryphius-Ginzberg-Ginsburg; I endured an interminable week (filled out with a tenuous false beard) in that perverse cubicle on the Rue de Toulon, until my friends spirited me away. From the running board one of them wrote on a pillar *The last of the letters of the Name has been spoken*. This sentence revealed that the series of crimes was *triple*. And the public thus understood it; nevertheless, I interspersed repeated signs that would allow you, Erik Lönnrot, the reasoner, to understand that it is *quadruple*. A portent in the North, others in the East and West, demand a fourth portent in the South; the Tetragrammaton —the name of God, JHVH—is made up of *four* letters; the harlequins and the paint shop sign suggested four points. In the manual of Leusden I underlined a certain passage: it manifested that the Hebrews calculate a day counting from dusk to dusk and that therefore the deaths occurred on the *fourth* day of each month. To Treviranus I sent the equilateral triangle. I sensed that you would supply the missing point. The point which would form a perfect rhomb, the point which fixes where death, exactly, awaits you. In order to attract you I have premeditated everything, Erik Lönnrot, so as to draw you to the solitude of Triste-le-Roy."

Lönnrot avoided Scharlach's eyes. He was looking at the trees and the sky divided into rhombs of turbid yellow, green, and red. He felt a little cold, and felt, too, an impersonal, almost anonymous sadness. It was already night; from the dusty garden arose the useless cry of a bird. For the last time, Lönnrot considered the problem of symmetrical and periodic death.

"In your labyrinth there are three lines too many," he said at last. "I know of a Greek labyrinth which is a single straight line. Along this line so many philosophers have lost themselves that a mere detective might well do so too. Scharlach, when, in some other incarnation you hunt me, feign to commit (or do commit) a crime at A, then a second crime at B, eight kilometers from A, then a third crime at C, four kilometers from A and B, halfway enroute between the two. Wait for me later at D, two kilometers from A and C, halfway, once again, between both. Kill me at D, as you are now going to kill me at Triste-le-Roy."

"The next time I kill you," said Scharlach, "I promise you the labyrinth made of the single straight line which is invisible and everlasting."

He stepped back a few paces. Then, very carefully, he fired.

—*Translated by* ANTHONY KERRIGAN

THE PLOT

To make his horror complete, Caesar, pursued to the base of a statue by the relentless daggers of his friends, discovers among the faces and blades the face of Marcus Junius Brutus, his favorite, his son perhaps, and he ceases to defend himself to exclaim: *"You too, my son!"* Shakespeare and Quevedo echo the pathetic cry.

Fate takes pleasure in repetitions, variants, symmetries. Nineteen centuries later, in the south of Buenos Aires province, a gaucho is assaulted by other gauchos, and, as he falls, recognizes a godson and with gentle reproach and gradual surprise exclaims (these words must be heard, not read): "But *che!*" He is killed and never knows he dies so that a scene may be re-enacted.

—Translated by ELAINE KERRIGAN

THE SOUTH

The man who landed in Buenos Aires in 1871 bore the name of Johannes Dahlmann and he was a minister in the Evangelical Church. In 1939, one of his grandchildren, Juan Dahlmann, was secretary of a municipal library on Calle Córdoba, and he considered himself profoundly Argentinian. His maternal grandfather had been that Francisco Flores, of the Second Line-Infantry Division, who had died on the frontier of Buenos Aires, run through with a lance by Indians from Catriel; in the discord inherent between his two lines of descent, Juan Dahlmann (perhaps driven to it by his Germanic blood) chose the line represented by his romantic ancestor, his ancestor of the romantic death. An old sword, a leather frame containing the daguerreotype of a blank-faced man with a beard, the dash and grace of certain music, the familiar strophes of *Martín Fierro*, the passing years, boredom and solitude, all went to foster this voluntary, but never ostentatious nationalism. At the cost of numerous small privations, Dahlmann had managed to save the empty shell of a ranch in the South which had belonged to the Flores family; he continually recalled the image of the balsamic eucalyptus trees and the great rose-colored house which had once been crimson. His duties, perhaps even indolence, kept him in the city. Summer after summer he contented himself with the abstract idea of possession and with the certitude that his ranch was waiting for him on a precise site in the middle of the plain. Late in February, 1939, something happened to him.

Blind to all fault, destiny can be ruthless at one's slightest distraction. Dahlmann had succeeded in acquiring, on that very afternoon, an imperfect copy of Weil's edition of *The Thousand and One Nights*. Avid to examine this find, he did

16

not wait for the elevator but hurried up the stairs. In the obscurity, something brushed by his forehead: a bat, a bird? On the face of the woman who opened the door to him he saw horror engraved, and the hand he wiped across his face came away red with blood. The edge of a recently painted door which someone had forgotten to close had caused this wound. Dahlmann was able to fall asleep, but from the moment he awoke at dawn the savor of all things was atrociously poignant. Fever wasted him and the pictures in *The Thousand and One Nights* served to illustrate nightmares. Friends and relatives paid him visits and, with exaggerated smiles, assured him that they thought he looked fine. Dahlmann listened to them with a kind of feeble stupor and he marveled at their not knowing that he was in hell. A week, eight days passed, and they were like eight centuries. One afternoon, the usual doctor appeared, accompanied by a new doctor, and they carried him off to a sanitarium on the Calle Ecuador, for it was necessary to X-ray him. Dahlmann, in the hackney coach which bore them away, thought that he would, at last, be able to sleep in a room different from his own. He felt happy and communicative. When he arrived at his destination, they undressed him, shaved his head, bound him with metal fastenings to a stretcher; they shone bright lights on him until he was blind and dizzy, auscultated him, and a masked man stuck a needle into his arm. He awoke with a feeling of nausea, covered with a bandage, in a cell with something of a well about it; in the days and nights which followed the operation he came to realize that he had merely been, up until then, in a suburb of hell. Ice in his mouth did not leave the least trace of freshness. During these days Dahlmann hated himself in minute detail: he hated his identity, his bodily necessities, his humiliation, the beard which bristled upon his face. He stoically endured the curative measures, which were painful, but when the surgeon told him he had been on the point of death from septicemia, Dahlmann dissolved in tears of self-pity for his fate. Physical wretchedness and the incessant anticipation of horrible nights had not allowed him time to think of anything so abstract as death. On another day, the surgeon told him he was healing and that, very soon, he would be able to go to his ranch for convalescence. Incredibly enough, the promised day arrived.

Reality favors symmetries and slight anachronisms: Dahlmann had arrived at the sanitarium in a hackney coach and now a hackney coach was to take him to the Constitución station. The first fresh tang of autumn, after the summer's oppressiveness, seemed like a symbol in nature of his rescue and release from fever and death. The city, at seven in the morning, had not lost that air of an old house lent it by the night; the streets seemed like long vestibules, the plazas were like patios. Dahlmann recognized the city with joy on the edge of vertigo: a second before his eyes registered the phenomena themselves, he recalled the corners, the billboards, the modest variety of Buenos Aires. In the yellow light of the new day, all things returned to him.

Every Argentine knows that the South begins at the other side of Rivadavia. Dahlmann was in the habit of saying that this was no mere convention, that whoever crosses this street enters a more ancient and sterner world. From inside the carriage he sought out, among the new buildings, the iron grille window, the brass knocker, the arched door, the entranceway, the intimate patio.

At the railroad station he noted that he still had thirty minutes. He quickly recalled that in a café on the Calle Brazil (a few dozen feet from Yrigoyen's house) there was an enormous cat which allowed itself to be caressed as if it were a disdainful divinity. He entered the café. There was the cat, asleep. He ordered a cup of coffee, slowly stirred the sugar, sipped it (this pleasure had been denied him in the clinic), and thought, as he smoothed the cat's black coat, that this contact was an illusion and that the two beings, man and cat, were as good as separated by a glass, for man lives in time, in succession, while the magical animal lives in the present, in the eternity of the instant.

Along the next to the last platform the train lay waiting. Dahlmann walked through the coaches until he found one almost empty. He arranged his baggage in the network rack. When the train started off, he took down his valise and extracted, after some hesitation, the first volume of *The Thousand and One Nights*. To travel with this book, which was so much a part of the history of his ill-fortune, was a kind of affirmation that his ill-fortune had been annulled; it was a joyous and secret defiance of the frustrated forces of evil.

Along both sides of the train the city dissipated into suburbs; this sight, and then a view of the gardens and villas, delayed the beginning of his reading. The truth was that Dahlmann read very little. The magnetized mountain and the genie who swore to kill his benefactor are—who would deny it?—marvelous, but not so much more than the morning itself and the mere fact of being. The joy of life distracted him from paying attention to Scheherazade and her superfluous miracles. Dahlmann closed his book and allowed himself to live.

Lunch—the bouillon served in shining metal bowls, as in the remote summers of childhood—was one more peaceful and rewarding delight.

Tomorrow I'll wake up at the ranch, he thought, and it was as if he was two men at a time: the man who traveled through the autumn day and across the geography of the fatherland, and the other one, locked up in a sanitarium and subject to methodical servitude. He saw unplastered brick houses, long and angled, timelessly watching the trains go by; he saw horsemen along the dirt roads; he saw gullies and lagoons and ranches; he saw great luminous clouds that resembled marble; and all these things were accidental, casual, like dreams of the plain. He also thought he recognized trees and crop fields; but he would not have been able to name them, for his actual knowledge of the countryside was quite inferior to his nostalgic and literary knowledge.

From time to time he slept, and his dreams were animated by the impetus of the train. The intolerable white sun of high noon had already become the yellow sun which precedes nightfall, and it would not be long before it would turn red. The railroad car was now also different; it was not the same as the one which had quit the station siding at Constitución; the plain and the hours had transfigured it. Outside, the moving shadow of the railroad car stretched toward the horizon. The elemental earth was not perturbed either by settlements or other signs of humanity. The country was vast but at the same time intimate and, in some measure, secret. The limitless country sometimes contained only a solitary bull. The solitude was perfect, perhaps hostile, and it might have occurred to Dahlmann that he was traveling into the past and not merely south. He was distracted from these considerations by the railroad inspector who, on reading his ticket, advised him that the train would not let him off at the regular station but at another: an earlier stop, one scarcely known to Dahlmann. (The man added an explanation which Dahlmann did not attempt to understand, and which he hardly heard, for the mechanism of events did not concern him.)

The train laboriously ground to a halt, practically in the middle of the plain. The station lay on the other side of the tracks; it was not much more than a siding and a shed. There was no means of conveyance to be seen, but the station chief supposed that the traveler might secure a vehicle from a general store and inn to be found some ten or twelve blocks away.

Dahlmann accepted the walk as a small adventure. The sun had already disappeared from view, but a final splendor exalted the vivid and silent plain, before the night erased its color. Less to avoid fatigue than to draw out his enjoyment of these sights, Dahlmann walked slowly, breathing in the odor of clover with sumptuous joy.

The general store at one time had been painted a deep scarlet, but the years had tempered this violent color for its own good. Something in its poor architecture recalled a steel engraving, perhaps one from an old edition of *Paul et Virginie*. A number of horses were hitched up to the paling. Once inside, Dahlmann thought he recognized the shopkeeper. Then he realized that he had been deceived by the man's resemblance to one of the male nurses in the sanitarium. When the shopkeeper heard Dahlmann's request, he said he would have the shay made up. In order to add one more event to that day and to kill time, Dahlmann decided to eat at the general store.

Some country louts, to whom Dahlmann did not at first pay any attention, were eating and drinking at one of the tables. On the floor, and hanging on to the bar, squatted an old man, immobile as an object. His years had reduced and polished him as water does a stone or the generations of men do a sentence. He was dark, dried up, diminutive, and seemed outside time, situated in eternity. Dahlmann noted with satisfaction the kerchief, the thick poncho, the long *chiripá*, and the colt boots, and told himself, as he recalled futile discussions with people from the Northern counties or from the province of Entre Rios, that gauchos like this no longer existed outside the South.

Dahlmann sat down next to the window. The darkness began overcoming the plain, but the odor and sound of the earth penetrated the iron bars of the window. The shop owner brought him sardines, followed by some roast meat. Dahlmann washed the meal down with several glasses of red wine. Idling, he relished the tart savor of the wine, and let his gaze, now grown somewhat drowsy, wander over the shop. A kerosene lamp hung from a beam. There were three customers at the other table: two of them appeared to be farm workers; the third man, whose features hinted at Chinese blood, was drinking with his hat on. Of a sudden, Dahlmann felt something brush lightly against his face. Next to the heavy glass of turbid wine, upon one of the stripes in the tablecloth, lay a spit ball of breadcrumb. That was all: but someone had thrown it there.

The men at the other table seemed totally cut off from him. Perplexed, Dahlmann decided that nothing had happened, and he opened the volume of *The Thousand and One Nights,* by way of suppressing reality. After a few moments another little ball landed on his table, and now the *peones* laughed outright. Dahlmann said to himself that he was not frightened, but he reasoned that it would be a major blunder if he, a convalescent, were to allow himself to be dragged by strangers into some chaotic quarrel. He determined to leave, and had already gotten to his feet when the owner came up and exhorted him in an alarmed voice:

"*Señor* Dahlmann, don't pay any attention to those lads; they're half high."

Dahlmann was not surprised to learn that the other man, now, knew his name. But he felt that these conciliatory words served only to aggravate the situation. Previously to this moment, the *peones'* provocation was directed against an unknown face, against no one in particular, almost against no one at all. Now it was an attack against him, against his name, and his neighbors knew it. Dahlmann pushed the owner aside, confronted the *peones,* and demanded to know what they wanted of him.

The tough with the Chinese look staggered heavily to his feet. Almost in Juan Dahlmann's face he shouted insults, as if he had been a long way off. His game was to exaggerate his drunkenness, and this extravagance constituted a ferocious mockery. Between curses and obscenities, he threw a long knife into the air, followed it with his eyes, caught and juggled it, and challenged Dahlmann to a knife fight. The owner objected in a tremulous voice, pointing out that Dahlmann was unarmed. At this point, something unforeseeable occurred.

From a corner of the room, the old ecstatic gaucho—in whom Dahlmann saw a summary and cipher of the South (his South)—threw him a naked dagger, which landed at his feet. It was as if the South had resolved that Dahlmann should accept the duel. Dahlmann bent over to pick up the dagger, and felt two things. The first, that this almost instinctive act bound him to fight. The second, that the weapon, in his torpid hand, was no defense at all, but would merely serve to justify his murder. He had once played with a poniard, like all men, but his idea of fencing and knife-play did not go further than the notion that all strokes should be directed upward, with the cutting edge held inward. *They would not have allowed such things to happen to me in the sanitarium*, he thought.

"Let's get on our way," said the other man.

They went out and if Dahlmann was without hope, he was also without fear. As he crossed the threshold, he felt that to die in a knife fight, under the open sky, and going forward to the attack, would have been a liberation, a joy, and a festive occasion, on the first night in the sanitarium, when they stuck him with the needle. He felt that if he had been able to choose, then, or to dream his death, this would have been the death he would have chosen or dreamt.

Firmly clutching his knife, which he perhaps would not know how to wield, Dahlmann went out into the plain.

—*Translated by* ANTHONY KERRIGAN

A PAGE TO COMMEMORATE COLONEL SUÁREZ, VICTOR AT JUNÍN

What do they matter now, the deprivations,
the alienation, the frustrations of growing old,
the dictator's shadow spreading across the land, the
    house
in the Barrio del Alto, which his brothers sold while
    he fought,
the useless days
(those one hopes to forget, those one knows are for-
    gettable),
when he had, at least, his burning hour, on horse-
    back
on the clear plains of Junín, a setting for the future?

What matters the flow of time, if he knew
that fullness, that ecstasy, that afternoon?

He served three years in the American Wars; and
    then
luck took him to Uruguay, to the banks of the Río
    Negro.
In the dying afternoons, he would think
that somehow, for him, a rose had burst into flower,
taken flesh in the battle of Junín, the ever-extending
    moment
when the lances clashed, the order which shaped the
    battle,
the initial defeat, and in the uproar
(no less harsh for him than for the army),

his voice crying out at the attacking Peruvians,
the light, the force, the fatefulness of the charge,
the teeming labyrinths of foot soldiers,
the crossing of lances, when no shot resounded,
the Spaniard fighting with a reckless sword,
the victory, the luck, the exhaustion, a dream begin-
    ning,
and the men dying among the swamps,
and Bolívar uttering words which were marked for
    history,
and the sun, in the west by now, and, anew, the taste
of wine and water,
and death, that death without a face,
for the battle had trampled over it, effaced it . . .

His great-grandson is writing these lines,
and a silent voice comes to him out of the past,
out of the blood:

"What does my battle at Junín matter if it is only
a glorious memory, or a date learned by rote
for an examination, or a place in the atlas?
The battle is everlasting, and can do without
the pomp of the obvious armies with their trumpets;
Junín is two civilians cursing a tyrant
on a street corner,
or an unknown man somewhere, dying in prison."

                —*Translated by* ALASTAIR REID

THE DEAD MAN

That a man from the suburbs of Buenos Aires, a wistful *compadrito,* with no other virtue than an infatuation with courage, should penetrate the equestrian wastelands along the Brazilian-Argentine frontier and become a captain of contrabandists would seem, initially, impossible. To those who think so, I should like to recount the story of Benjamín Otálora, of whom there is probably not so much as a memory left in the Balvanera quarter, and who died according to his own law, from a bullet, on the borders of Río Grande do Sul. I do not know the details of his adventure; when they are given me, I shall rectify and amplify these pages. For the moment, the following résumé may serve.

In about 1891, Benjamín Otálora is nineteen years old. He is a bully with a low brow, ingenuous light eyes and Basque robustness. A lucky knife thrust has revealed to him that he is brave; the death of his opponent does not disquiet him, nor does the immediate need to flee the Argentine. The boss of his parish gives him a letter for a certain Azevedo Bandeira, of Uruguay. Otálora embarks; the crossing is stormy and the ship works hard; the next day he wanders through the streets of Montevideo with unconfessed and perhaps even unconscious sadness. He does not find Azevedo Bandeira; toward midnight, in a dive on the Paso del Molino, he is witness to an altercation between a number of cattle drovers. A knife flashes; Otálora does not know which side is in the right but he is attracted by the pure taste of danger, as others are attracted by playing cards or music. In the confusion he fends off a low knife thrust by a *peón* against a man wearing a dark slouch hat and a poncho. This man turns out to be Azevedo Bandeira. (When Otálora

26

finds out, he tears up the letter to him, preferring to owe everything to himself.) Though husky, Azevedo Bandeira gives an unjustified impression of being deformed; in his face, always looming too close, are the Jew, the Negro, and the Indian; in his look, the monkey and the tiger; the scar which cuts across his face is one more ornament, like his black bristly mustache.

The altercation—a projection or error of alcohol—comes to an end with the same rapidity with which it began. Otálora drinks with the drovers and later accompanies them to a party, and still later to a big house in the Old City, the sun by now high in the sky. In the innermost patio, which is of earth, the men spread out their gear to sleep on. Otálora dimly compares this night with the previous one: now he walks on solid ground, among friends. True, he feels a bit uneasy that he does not miss Buenos Aires. He sleeps until the hour for morning prayer, when he is awakened by the countryman who had drunkenly attacked Bandeira. (Otálora recalls that this man shared with the others the tumultuous and jubilant night and that Bandeira sat him down at his right and obliged him to go on drinking.) The man tells him that the Chief has sent for him. In a kind of office leading into the entranceway (Otálora had never seen an entranceway with lateral doors), Azevedo Bandeira is awaiting him, in the company of a fine disdainful woman with red hair. Bandeira appraises him, offers him a shot of cane brandy, repeats that Otálora strikes him as a brave man, proposes he go north with the rest of them to bring back a herd. Otálora accepts; toward dawn they are on the road, en route to Tacuarembó.

Otálora now begins a different life, a life of vast dawns and of days smelling of horses. It is a new life for him, sometimes an atrocious one, but it has already passed into his bloodstream, for just as men of other nations venerate

and feel a presentiment of the sea, in the same way we
Argentines (including the man who interweaves these symbols) long for the inexhaustible plains which resound beneath the hooves. Otálora was raised in the quarter of the
city inhabited by carters and wagoners; before a year is
out, he has become a gaucho. He learns to ride, to round up
the cattle on the hacienda, to slaughter on the range, to
handle the lasso and the bolas that fell cattle, to fight off
sleep, to endure storms and frost and sun, to drive live-
stock with whistles and cries. Only once in all this time of
apprenticeship does he see Azevedo Bandeira, but the latter
is very much in his mind, for to be *one of Bandeira's men*
is to be highly considered and feared, and because, in the
face of any and all manliness, the gauchos say "Bandeira
does it better." Someone asserts that Bandeira was born on
the other side of the Cuareim, in Río Grande do Sul: this
attribution, which should make him less, adds a dimension
and mysteriously leagues him with thick jungles, with
swamps, with inextricable and almost infinite distances.
Gradually, Otálora realizes that Bandeira's affairs are
multiple and that chief among them is smuggling. To be a
cattle drover is to be a serf; Otálora determines to rise to the
rank of contrabandist. One night, two comrades are to cross
the frontier and bring back a quantity of cane brandy;
Otálora picks a quarrel with one of them, wounds him, and
then takes his place. He is moved to it by ambition, and
also by some dark sense of loyalty. *Let that man* (he
thinks) *realize, once and for all, that I'm worth more than
all his Uruguayans put together.*

A year passes before Otálora returns to Montevideo. The
party rides along the river bank, around the city (which
strikes Otálora as immense); they arrive at the Chief's
house; the men spread out their gear in the inmost patio.
The days pass and Otálora still has not seen Bandeira. They

say, fearfully, that he is sick; a mulatto customarily takes up his soup caldron and his maté tea to his quarters. One afternoon, Otálora is entrusted with the job. He feels a vague humiliation, but also satisfaction.

The bedroom is dilapidated and dark. There is a balcony facing west, a long table covered with whips, horsewhips, gun and cartridge belts, firearms and knives, and there is a remote mirror with its glass dimmed. Bandeira lies face upward; he dreams and moans; the vehemence of a final sun outlines him. The vast white bed seems to diminish and obscure him; Otálora takes note of the gray hair, the fatigue, the flaccidity, the fissures of the years. He is revolted at the thought that this old man should be their leader. It occurs to him that a single blow would be enough to take care of the man in the bed. At this juncture he notices in the mirror that someone has come into the room. It is the red-haired woman; she is half-dressed and barefoot, and she observes him with cold curiosity. Bandeira sits up; while he talks of country matters and drinks one maté after another, his fingers play with the woman's braids. At last, he gives Otálora permission to withdraw.

Days later, the order to go north is given. They ride to a lost far-off country house, which stands as it might have stood in any other part whatsoever of the interminable plain. Neither trees nor a stream gladden it; the first sun and the last beat upon it. The hacienda boasts stone corrals, but the whole place is run down. This poor place is called *The Sigh*.

Otálora learns, from a discussion among the *peones*, that Bandeira will soon be coming from Montevideo. He asks why, and is told that there is an outsider among them, an outsider-turned-gaucho who is trying to take over. Otálara realizes that they are joking, but he is flattered that such a joke has become possible. He learns, a bit later, that

Bandeira has fallen out with one of the political chieftains and that the latter has withdrawn his support. This news pleases him.

Boxes of long weapons begin to arrive; a silver jar and basin arrive for the woman's quarters; intricate damask curtains arrive; out of the mountain range, one morning, rides a somber horseman, with a heavy beard and wearing a poncho. His name is Ulpiano Suárez, and he is Azevedo Bandeira's *capanga* or bodyguard. He says little and speaks with Brazilian intonations. Otálora does not know whether to attribute his reserve to hostility, scorn, or mere barbarity. He does know, for sure, that in order to carry out the plan he is hatching, he must gain his favor.

A reddish horse with black points next enters into Benjamín Otálora's destiny; it is brought from the South by Azevedo Bandeira, and it boasts accouterments covered with metal and saddle padding bordered with tiger skin. This free-spirited horse is a symbol of the Chief's authority, and for that reason the boy covets it; he also desires, with a rancorous desire, the woman with the luminous hair. The woman, the accouterments, and the reddish horse are attributes or adjectives of a man whom he aspires to destroy.

Here the story becomes complicated, more profound. Azevedo Bandeira is an expert in the art of progressive intimidation, in the satanic maneuver of gradually humiliating his interlocutor by combining verities and gibes; Otálora resolves to apply this ambiguous method to the hard task he has set himself. He resolves to supplant, slowly, Azevedo Bandeira. He gains, during days of common danger, the friendship of Suárez. He confides in him his plan; Suárez promises his help. Many things happen thereafter, a small number of which I know about. Otálora does not carry out Bandeira's orders: he overlooks them, corrects them, invents them. The entire universe seems to conspire along with him, and to hasten events. One noonday, in some fields

in Tacuarembó, there is an exchange of gunfire with a gang
from Río Grande province; Otálora usurps Bandeira's place
and takes command of the Uruguayans. A bullet goes
through his shoulder, but that afternoon Otálora rides back
to *The Sigh* on the red horse of the Chief, and that afternoon some drops of his blood stain the tiger skin, and that
night he sleeps with the woman with the luminous hair.
Other versions of the story change the order of these events
and even deny that they all occurred in one day.

Bandeira, nevertheless, is always nominally Chief. He
issues orders which are not executed. Benjamín Otálora
does not touch him, for mixed reasons of custom and pity.

The last scene of the drama corresponds to the upheaval
of the last night. That night, the men at *The Sigh* eat
freshly slaughtered meat, and drink a fighting liquor; someone infinitely draws out flourishes of an elaborate *milonga*
on the guitar. At the head of the table, Otálora, drunk,
adds exultation to exultation, jubilation to jubilation; this
vertiginous tower becomes a symbol of his irresistible
destiny. Bandeira, taciturn among the shouters, lets the
night flow clamorously along. When the bell tolls twelve, he
rises like a man remembering an obligation. He gets up and
knocks softly at the woman's door. She opens to him
swiftly, as if she had been awaiting his call. She comes out
half-dressed and barefoot. In a voice grown effeminate, a
voice which comes thickly, the Chief gives an order:

"Now that you and the man from Buenos Aires are
so much in love, you can go and give him a kiss right in
front of everybody."

He adds a brutal particular, an obscene detail. The
woman tries to resist, but two men take her by the arm and
push her upon Otálora. Dissolving in tears, she kisses his
face and chest. Ulpiano Suárez has taken his revolver in his
hand. Otálora realizes before he dies, that they have
betrayed him from the start, that he has been condemned to

death; that they have allowed him to make love, to command, to triumph, because they had already given him up for dead, because in Bandeira's eyes he was already dead.

Suárez, almost scornfully, pulls the trigger.

—*Translated by* Anthony Kerrigan

MATTHEW 25:30

And cast ye the unprofitable servant into outer darkness:
there shall be weeping and gnashing of teeth.

The first bridge on Constitución. At my feet
the shunting trains trace iron labyrinths.
Steam hisses up and up into the night
which becomes, at a stroke, the Night of the Last
    Judgment.

From the unseen horizon,
and from the very center of my being,
an infinite voice pronounced these things—
things, not words. This is my feeble translation,
time-bound, of what was a single limitless Word:

"Stars, bread, libraries of East and West,
playing cards, chessboards, galleries, skylights,
    cellars,
a human body to walk with on the earth,
fingernails, growing at nighttime and in death,
shadows for forgetting, mirrors which endlessly
    multiply,
falls in music, gentlest of all time's shapes,
borders of Brazil, Uruguay, horses and mornings,
a bronze weight, a copy of Grettir Saga,
algebra and fire, the charge at Junín in your blood,
days more crowded than Balzac, scent of the honey-
    suckle,
love, and the imminence of love, and intolerable
    remembering,
dreams like buried treasure, generous luck,
and memory itself, where a glance can make men
    dizzy—

all this was given to you and, with it,
the ancient nourishment of heroes—
treachery, defeat, humiliation.
In vain have oceans been squandered on you, in
    vain
the sun, wonderfully seen through Whitman's eyes.
You have used up the years and they have used up
    you,
and still, and still, you have not written the poem."

            —*Translated by* ALASTAIR REID

FUNES, THE MEMORIOUS

I remember him (I scarcely have the right to use this ghostly verb; only one man on earth deserved the right, and he is dead), I remember him with a dark passionflower in his hand, looking at it as no one has ever looked at such a flower, though they might look from the twilight of day until the twilight of night, for a whole life long. I remember him, his face immobile and Indian-like, and singularly *remote*, behind his cigarette. I remember (I believe) the strong delicate fingers of the plainsman who can braid leather. I remember, near those hands, a vessel in which to make maté tea, bearing the arms of the Banda Oriental;* I remember, in the window of the house, a yellow rush mat, and beyond, a vague marshy landscape. I remember clearly his voice, the deliberate, resentful, nasal voice of the old eastern shore man, without the Italianate sibilants of today. I did not see him more than three times; the last time, in 1887. . . .

That all those who knew him should write something about him seems to me a very felicitous idea; my testimony may perhaps be the briefest and without doubt the poorest, and it will not be the least impartial. The deplorable fact of my being an Argentinian will hinder me from falling into a dithyramb—an obligatory form in the Uruguay, when the theme is an Uruguayan.

Littérateur, slicker, Buenos Airean: Funes did not use these insulting phrases, but I am sufficiently aware that for him I represented these unfortunate categories. Pedro Leandro Ipuche has written that Funes was a precursor of the superman, "an untamed and vernacular Zarathustra"; I do

---

* The eastern shore of the Uruguay River; now the Orient Republic of Uruguay.—*Editor's note.*

not doubt it, but one must not forget, either, that he was a countryman from the town of Fray Bentos, with certain incurable limitations.

My first recollection of Funes is quite clear, I see him at dusk, sometime in March or February of the year '84. That year, my father had taken me to spend the summer at Fray Bentos. I was on my way back from the farm at San Francisco with my cousin Bernardo Haedo. We came back singing, on horseback; and this last fact was not the only reason for my joy. After a sultry day, an enormous slate-gray storm had obscured the sky. It was driven on by a wind from the south; the trees were already tossing like madmen; and I had the apprehension (the secret hope) that the elemental downpour would catch us out in the open. We were running a kind of race with the tempest. We rode into a narrow lane which wound down between two enormously high brick footpaths. It had grown black of a sudden; I now heard rapid, almost secret steps above; I raised my eyes and saw a boy running along the narrow, cracked path as if he were running along a narrow, broken wall. I remember the loose trousers, tight at the bottom, the hemp sandals; I remember the cigarette in the hard visage, standing out against the by now limitless darkness. Bernardo unexpectedly yelled to him: "What's the time, Ireneo?" Without looking up, without stopping, Ireneo replied: "In ten minutes it will be eight o'clock, child Bernardo Juan Francisco." The voice was sharp, mocking.

I am so absent-minded that the dialogue which I have just cited would not have penetrated my attention if it had not been repeated by my cousin, who was stimulated, I think, by a certain local pride and by a desire to show himself indifferent to the other's three-sided reply.

He told me that the boy above us in the pass was a certain Ireneo Funes, renowned for a number of eccentricities, such as that of having nothing to do with people and of always knowing the time, like a watch. He added that Ireneo was the son of María Clementina Funes, an ironing woman in the town, and that his father, some people said, was an "Englishman" named O'Connor, a doctor in the salting fields, though some said the father was a horse-breaker, or scout, from the province of El Salto. Ireneo lived with his mother, at the edge of the country house of the Laurels.

In the years '85 and '86 we spent the summer in the city of Montevideo. We returned to Fray Bentos in '87. As was natural, I inquired after all my acquaintances, and finally, about "the chronometer Funes." I was told that he had been thrown by a wild horse at the San Francisco ranch, and that he had been hopelessly crippled. I remember the impression of uneasy magic which the news provoked in me: the only time I had seen him we were on horseback, coming from San Francisco, and he was in a high place; from the lips of my cousin Bernardo the affair sounded like a dream elaborated with elements out of the past. They told me that Ireneo did not move now from his cot, but remained with his eyes fixed on the backyard fig tree, or on a cobweb. At sunset he allowed himself to be brought to the window. He carried pride to the extreme of pretending that the blow which had befallen him was a good thing. . . . Twice I saw him behind the iron grate which sternly delineated his eternal imprisonment: unmoving, once, his eyes closed; unmoving also, another time, absorbed in the contemplation of a sweet-smelling sprig of lavender cotton.

At the time I had begun, not without some ostentation, the methodical study of Latin. My valise contained the *De viris illustribus* of Lhomond, the *Thesaurus* of Quicherat, Caesar's *Commentaries,* and an odd-numbered volume of the *Historia Naturalis* of Pliny, which exceeded (and still exceeds) my modest talents as a Latinist. Everything is noised around in a small town; Ireneo, at his small farm on the outskirts, was not long in learning of the arrival of these anomalous books. He sent me a flowery, ceremonious letter, in which he recalled our encounter, unfortunately brief, "on the seventh day of February of the year '84," and alluded to the glorious services which Don Gregorio Haedo, my uncle, dead the same year, "had rendered to the Two Fatherlands in the glorious campaign of Ituzaingó," and he solicited the loan of any one of the volumes, to be accompanied by a dictionary "for the better intelligence of the original text, for I do not know Latin as yet." He promised to return them in good condition, almost immediately. The letter was perfect, very nicely constructed; the orthography was of the type sponsored by Andrés Bello: *i* for *y, j* for *g*. At first I naturally suspected a jest. My cousins assured me it was not so, that these were the ways of Ireneo. I did not know whether to attribute to impudence, ignorance, or stupidity, the idea that the difficult Latin required no other instrument than a dictionary; in order fully to undeceive him I sent the *Gradus ad Parnassum* of Quicherat, and the Pliny.

On February 14, I received a telegram from Buenos Aires telling me to return immediately, for my father was "in no way well." God forgive me, but the prestige of being the recipient of an urgent telegram, the desire to point out to all of Fray Bentos the contradiction between the negative form of the news and the positive adverb, the temptation to dramatize my sorrow as I feigned a virile stoicism, all no doubt distracted me from the possibility of anguish. As I packed my valise, I noted that I was missing the *Gradus* and the volume of the *Historia Naturalis*. The "Saturn" was to weigh anchor on the morning of the next day; that night, after supper, I made my way to the house of Funes. Outside, I was surprised to find the night no less oppressive than the day.

Ireneo's mother received me at the modest ranch. She told me that Ireneo was in the back room and that

I should not be disturbed to find him in the dark, for he knew how to pass the dead hours without lighting the candle. I crossed the cobblestone patio, the small corridor; I came to the second patio. A great vine covered everything, so that the darkness seemed complete. Of a sudden I heard the high-pitched, mocking voice of Ireneo. The voice spoke in Latin; the voice (which came out of the obscurity) was reading, with obvious delight, a treatise or prayer or incantation. The Roman syllables resounded in the earthen patio; my suspicion made them seem undecipherable, interminable; afterward, in the enormous dialogue of that night, I learned that they made up the first paragraph of the twenty-fourth chapter of the seventh book of the *Historia Naturalis*. The subject of this chapter is memory; the last words are *ut nihil non iisdem verbis redderetur auditum.*

Without the least change in his voice, Ireneo bade me come in. He was lying on the cot, smoking. It seems to me that I did not see his face until dawn; I seem to recall the momentary glow of the cigarette. The room smelled vaguely of dampness. I sat down, and repeated the story of the telegram and my father's illness.

I come now to the most difficult point in my narrative. For the entire story has no other point (the reader might as well know it by now) than this dialogue of almost a half-century ago. I shall not attempt to reproduce his words, now irrecoverable. I prefer truthfully to make a résumé of the many things Ireneo told me. The indirect style is remote and weak; I know that I sacrifice the effectiveness of my narrative; but let my readers imagine the nebulous sentences which clouded that night.

Ireneo began by enumerating, in Latin and Spanish, the cases of prodigious memory cited in the *Historia Naturalis:* Cyrus, king of the Persians, who could call every soldier in his armies by name; Mithridates Eupator, who administered justice in the twenty-two languages of his empire; Simonides, inventor of mnemotechny; Metrodorus, who practiced the art of repeating faithfully what he heard once. With evident good faith Funes marveled that such things should be considered marvelous. He told me that previous to the rainy afternoon when the blue-tinted horse threw him, he had been—like any Christian—blind, deaf, mute, somnambulistic, memoryless. (I tried to remind him of his precise perception of time, his memory for proper names; he paid no attention to me.) For nineteen years, he said, he had lived like a person in a dream: he looked without seeing, heard without hearing, forgot everything—almost everything. On falling from the horse, he lost consciousness; when he recovered it, the present was almost intolerable it was so rich and bright; the same was true of the most ancient and most trivial memories. A little later he realized that he was crippled. This fact scarcely interested him. He reasoned (or felt) that immobility was a minimum price to pay. And now, his perception and his memory were infallible.

We, in a glance, perceive three wine glasses on the table; Funes saw all the shoots, clusters, and grapes of the vine. He remembered the shapes of the clouds in the south at dawn on the 30th of April of 1882, and he could compare them in his recollection with the marbled grain in the design of a leather-bound book which he had seen only once, and with the lines in the spray which an oar raised in the Río Negro on the eve of the battle of the Quebracho. These recollections were not simple; each visual image was linked to muscular sensations, thermal sensations, etc. He could reconstruct all his dreams, all his fancies. Two or three times he had reconstructed an entire day. He told me: *I have more memories in myself alone than all men have had since the world was a world.* And again: *My dreams are like your vigils.* And again, toward dawn: *My memory, sir, is like a garbage disposal.*

A circumference on a blackboard, a rectangular triangle, a rhomb, are forms which we can fully intuit; the same held true with Ireneo for the tempestuous mane of a stallion, a herd of cattle in a pass, the ever-changing flame or the innumerable ash, the many faces of a dead man during the course of a protracted wake. He could perceive I do not know how many stars in the sky.

These things he told me; neither then nor at any time later did they seem doubtful. In those days neither the cinema nor the phonograph yet existed; nevertheless, it seems strange, almost incredible, that no one should have experimented on Funes. The truth is that we all live by leaving behind; no doubt we all profoundly know that we are immortal and that sooner or later every man will do all things and know everything.

The voice of Funes, out of the darkness, continued. He told me that toward 1886 he had devised a new system of enumeration and that in a very few days he had gone beyond twenty-four thousand. He had not written it down, for what he once meditated would not be erased. The first stimulus to his work, I believe, had been his discontent with the fact that "thirty-three Uruguayans" required two symbols and three words, rather than a single word and a single symbol. Later he applied his extravagant principle to the other numbers. In place of seven thousand thirteen, he would say (for example) *Máximo Perez;* in place of seven thousand fourteen, *The Train;* other numbers were *Luis Melián Lafinur, Olimar, Brimstone, Clubs, The Whale, Gas, The Caldron, Napoleon, Augustin de Vedia.* In lieu of five hundred, he would say *nine.* Each word had a particular sign, a species of mark; the last were very complicated. . . . I attempted to explain that this rhapsody of unconnected terms was precisely the contrary of a system of enumeration. I said that to say three hundred and sixty-five was to say three hundreds, six tens, five units: an analysis which does not exist in such numbers as *The Negro Timoteo* or *The Flesh Blanket*. Funes did not understand me, or did not wish to understand me.

Locke, in the seventeenth century, postulated (and rejected) an impossible idiom in which each individual object, each stone, each bird and branch had an individual name; Funes had once projected an analogous idiom, but he had renounced it as being too general, too ambiguous. In effect, Funes not only remembered every leaf on every tree of every wood, but even every one of the times he had perceived or imagined it. He determined to reduce all of his past experience to some seventy thousand recollections, which he would later define numerically. Two considerations dissuaded him: the thought that the task was interminable and the thought that it was useless. He knew that at the hour of his death he would scarcely have finished classifying even all the memories of his childhood.

The two projects I have indicated (an infinite vocabulary for the natural series of numbers, and a usable mental catalogue of all the images of memory) are lacking in sense, but they reveal a certain stammering greatness. They allow us to make out dimly, or to infer, the dizzying world of Funes. He was, let us not forget, almost incapable of general, platonic ideas. It was not only difficult for him to understand that the generic term *dog* embraced so many unlike specimens of differing sizes and different forms; he was disturbed by the fact that a dog at three-fourteen (seen in profile) should have the same name as the dog at three-fifteen (seen from the front). His own face in the mirror, his own hands, surprised him on every occasion. Swift writes that the emperor of Lilliput could discern the movement of the minute hand; Funes could continuously make out the tranquil advances of corruption, of caries, of fatigue. He noted the progress of death, of moisture. He was the solitary and lucid spectator of a multiform world which was instantaneously and almost intolerably exact. Babylon,

London, and New York have overawed the imagination of men with their ferocious splendor; no one, in those populous towers or upon those surging avenues, has felt the heat and pressure of a reality as indefatigable as that which day and night converged upon the unfortunate Ireneo in his humble South American farmhouse. It was very difficult for him to sleep. To sleep is to be abstracted from the world; Funes, on his back in his cot, in the shadows, imagined every crevice and every molding of the various houses which surrounded him. (I repeat, the least important of his recollections was more minutely precise and more lively than our perception of a physical pleasure or a physical torment.) Toward the east, in a section which was not yet cut into blocks of homes, there were some new unknown houses. Funes imagined them black, compact, made of a single obscurity; he would turn his face in this direction in order to sleep. He would also imagine himself at the bottom of the river, being rocked and annihilated by the current.

Without effort, he had learned English, French, Portuguese, Latin. I suspect, nevertheless, that he was not very capable of thought. To think is to forget a difference, to generalize, to abstract. In the overly replete world of Funes there were nothing but details, almost contiguous details.

The equivocal clarity of dawn penetrated along the earthen patio.

Then it was that I saw the face of the voice which had spoken all through the night. Ireneo was nineteen years old; he had been born in 1868; he seemed as monumental as bronze, more ancient than Egypt, anterior to the prophecies and the pyramids. It occurred to me that each one of my words (each one of my gestures) would live on in his implacable memory; I was benumbed by the fear of multiplying superfluous gestures.

Ireneo Funes died in 1889, of a pulmonary congestion.

—Translated by ANTHONY KERRIGAN

A NEW REFUTATION
OF TIME

Vor mir keine Zeit, nach mir wird keine seyn.
Mit mir gebiert sie sich, mit mir geht sie auch ein.

—Daniel von Czepko,
Sexcenta Monidisticha Sapientum. III, II (1655).

PROLOGUE

Had this refutation (or even the title) been published in
the middle of the eighteenth century, it would survive in
Hume's bibliographies or might even have merited a line by
Huxley or Kemp Smith. But published in 1947—post-
Bergson— it is an anachronistic *reductio ad absurdum* of a
preterite system or, what is worse, the feeble artifice of an
Argentinian gone astray in the maze of metaphysics. Both
conjectures are credible and perhaps even true: I can not
promise, so as to emend them, a startling resolution in exchange for my rudimentary dialectic. The thesis which I
shall expound is as old as Zeno's arrow or the chariot of the
Greek king in the *Milinda Panha;* its novelty, if any, consists in applying to my ends the classic instrument of
Berkeley. Both he and his continuer, David Hume, abound
in paragraphs which contradict or exclude my thesis; nevertheless, I believe I have deduced the inevitable consequence
of their doctrine.

The first article (A) was written in 1944 and appeared
in Number 115 of the Argentine magazine *Sur;* the second,
dating from 1946, is a revision of the first piece. I deliberately refrained from making the two into one, in the

belief that the reading of two analogous texts could facilitate the comprehension of intractable matter.

A word on the title: I am not oblivious of the fact that it is an example of the monster the logicians call *contradictio in adjecto,* for to say that a refutation of time is new (or old, for that matter) is to attribute to it a temporal predicate, thus restoring at once the very notion the subject strives to destroy. Still and all I shall let it stand, so that its ever-so-slight mockery give proof that I do not overrate the importance of this play on words. And then, too, our language is so thoroughly saturated and animated with the notion of time that quite possibly not a single sentence in all these pages fails to require or invoke it.

I dedicate these exercises to my ancestor Juan Crisóstomo Lafinur (1797–1824), who left a memorable hendecasyllable or two to Argentine letters and who strove to reform the teaching of philosophy by purifying it of theological shadows and explaining the theories of Locke and Condillac in his courses. He died in exile: it was his lot, as it is the lot of all men, to live in bad times.

A

I

In the course of a life dedicated to belles-lettres and, occasionally, to the perplexities of metaphysics, I have glimpsed or foreseen a refutation of time, one in which I myself do not believe, but which tends to visit me at night and in the hours of weary twilight, with the illusory force of an axiom. This refutation is to be found, in one form or another, in all of my books: it is prefigured in the poems *"Inscripción en cualquier sepulcro"* and *"El truco"* from my *Fervor de Buenos Aires* (1923); it is openly stated in two articles in my *Inquisiciones* (1925), on page 46 of the 1930 edition of *Evaristo Carriego,* in the story *"Sentirse en muerte*" from my *Historia de la eternidad* (1936), on page 46 of the 1942 edition of my book *El jardín de senderos que se bifurcan*. None of these texts satisfies me, not even the penultimate one in the list, which is less demonstrative and reasoned than divinatory and inclined toward pathos. I will attempt, by the present writing, to establish a basis for all of them.

Two arguments led me to this refutation of time: the idealism of Berkeley and Leibnitz' principle of indiscernibles. Berkeley (in *Principles of Human Knowledge*, 3) observed: "That neither our thoughts, nor passions, nor ideas formed by the imagination, exist without the mind, is what everybody will allow. And it seems no less evident that the various sensations or ideas imprinted on the sense, however blended or combined together (that is, whatever objects they compose), cannot exist otherwise than in a mind perceiving them. . . . The table I write on I say exists—that is, I see and feel it; and if I were out of my study I should say it existed—meaning thereby that if I was in my study I might perceive it, or that some other spirit actually does perceive it. . . . For as to what is said of the absolute existence of unthinking things without any relation to their being perceived, that seems perfectly unintelligible. Their *esse* is *percipi*, nor is it possible they should have any existence out of the minds or thinking things which perceive them."

In Paragraph 23 he added, foreseeing objections: "But, say you, surely there is nothing easier than for me to imagine trees, for instance, in a park, or books existing in a closet, and nobody by to perceive them. I answer, you may say so, there is no difficulty in it; but what is all this, I beseech you, more than framing in your mind certain ideas which you call *books* and *trees*, and at the same time omitting to frame the idea of any one that may perceive them? But do not you yourself perceive or think of them all the while?

This therefore is nothing to the purpose; it only shews you have the power of imagining or forming ideas in your mind: but it doth not shew that you can conceive it possible the objects of your thought may exist without the mind. . . ."

In another paragraph, Number 6, he had already declared: "Some truths there are so near and obvious to the mind that a man need only open his eyes to see them. Such I take this important one to be, to wit, that all the choir of heaven and furniture of the earth, in a word all those bodies which compose the mighty frame of the world, have not any subsistence without a mind, that their *being* is to be perceived or known; that consequently so long as they are not actually perceived by me, or do not exist in my mind or that of any other created spirit, they must either have no existence at all, or else subsist in the mind of some Eternal Spirit. . . ."

Such is, in the words of its inventor, the idealist doctrine. To understand it is easy; the difficulty lies in thinking within its limitations. Schopenhauer himself, in expounding it, is guilty of some culpable negligence. In the first lines of his book *Die Welt als Wille und Vorstellung*—dating from the year of 1819—he formulates the following declaration, which makes him a creditor as regards the sum total of imperishable human perplexity: "The world is my representation. The man who confesses this truth clearly understands that he does not know a sun nor an earth, but only some eyes which see a sun and a hand which feels an earth." That is, for the idealist Schopenhauer a man's eyes and hands are less illusory or unreal than the earth or the sun. In 1844, he publishes a complementary volume. In the very first chapter he rediscovers and aggravates the previous error: he defines the universe as a cerebral phenomenon, and he distinguishes between the "word in the head" and the "world outside the head." Berkeley, nevertheless, will have made his Philonous say, in 1713: "The brain therefore you speak of, being a sensible thing, exists only in the mind.

Now, I would fain know whether you think it reasonable to suppose, that one idea or thing existing in the mind, occasions all other ideas. And if you think so, pray how do you account for the origin of that primary idea or brain itself?" To Schopenhauer's dualism, or cerebralism, Spiller's monism may legitimately be counterposed. Spiller (in *The Mind of Man*, Ch. VIII, 1902) argues that the retina and the cutaneous surface invoked to explain visual and tactile phenomena are, in turn, two tactile and visual systems, and that the room we see (the "objective" one) is no greater than the imagined ("cerebral") one, and that the former does not contain the latter, since there are two independent visual systems involved. Berkeley (in *Principles of Human Knowledge*, 10 and 116) likewise denied primary qualities— the solidity and extension of things—or the existence of absolute space.

Berkeley affirmed the continuous existence of objects, inasmuch as when no individual perceives them, God does. Hume, with greater logic, denies this existence (in *Treatise of Human Nature*, I, 4, 2). Berkeley affirmed personal identity, "for I myself am not my ideas, but somewhat else, a thinking active principle that perceives" (*Dialogues*, 3). Hume, the skeptic, refutes this belief, and makes each man "a bundle or collection of different perceptions, which succeed each other with an inconceivable rapidity" (*op. cit.*, I, 4,6). Both men affirmed the existence of time: for Berkeley it is "the succession of ideas in my mind, which flows uniformly, and is participated in by all beings" (*Principles of Human Knowledge*, 98). For Hume, it is "a succession of indivisible moments" (*op. cit.*, I, 2,2).

I have here accumulated citations from the apologists of idealism, I have been prodigal with passages from their canon, I have been reiterative and explicit, I have censured Schopenhauer (not without ingratitude), all so that my reader may gradually penetrate this unstable world of the mind: a world of evanescent impressions; a world without matter or spirit, neither objective nor subjective; a world without the ideal architecture of space; a world made of time, of the absolute uniform time of the *Principia;* an indefatigable labyrinth, a chaos, a dream. It was to this almost perfect disintegration that David Hume was led.

Once the idealist argument is accepted, I understand that it is possible—perhaps inevitable—to go even further. For Hume, it is not licit to speak of the form of the moon or its color: its form and color *are* the moon. Neither can one speak of the mind's perceptions, inasmuch as the mind is nothing but a series of perceptions. The Cartesian "I think, therefore I am" is thus invalidated: to say *I think* is to postulate the I, and is a *petitio principii.* In the eighteenth century, Lichtenberg proposed that in place of *I think,* we should say, impersonally, *it thinks,* just as one could say *it thunders* or *it flashes* (lightning). I repeat: there is not, behind the visages, a secret *I* governing our acts and receiving our impressions. We are, merely, the series of those imaginary acts and those errant impressions. The series? Once matter and spirit—which are *continua*—are denied, once space is denied, I don't see what right we have to that *continuum* which is time. Let us imagine a present moment, any one at all. A night on the Mississippi. Huckleberry Finn wakes up. The raft, lost in the semi-obscurity, continues on downstream. It may be a bit cold. Huckleberry Finn recognizes the soft indefatigable sound of the water. Negligently he opens his eyes: he sees an indefinite number of stars, a nebulous line which is that of the trees. Then he sinks into a memoryless sleep, as into dark water.* Metaphysical idealism declares that to add to these perceptions a material sub-

---

* For the convenience of the reader I have chosen a moment between two intervals of sleep: a literary, not a historical, instant. If anyone suspects a fallacy, he can insert another example, one from his own life, if he wants.

stance (the object) and a spiritual substance (the subject) is venturesome and vain. I maintain that it is no less illogical to think that they are terms in a series whose beginning is as inconceivable as its end. To add to the river and the river bank perceived by Huck the notion of yet another substantive river with another river bank, to add yet another perception to that immediate network of perceptions is altogether unjustifiable in the eyes of idealism. In my eyes, it is no less unjustifiable to add a chronological precision: for instance, the fact that the above-mentioned event should have taken place on the night of June 7, 1849, between 4:10 and 4:11. To put it in other words: I deny, using the arguments of idealism, the vast temporal series which idealism allows. Hume denied the existence of an absolute space, in which each thing has its place; I deny the existence of one single time, in which all events are linked. To deny coexistence is no less difficult than to deny succession.

I deny, in a high number of instances, the existence of succession. I deny, in a high number of instances, contemporaneity as well. The lover who thinks *While I was so happy, thinking of my love's faithfulness, she was busy deceiving me,* is deceiving himself. If every state in which we live is absolute, that happiness was not contemporary to that betrayal. The discovery of that betrayal is merely one more state, incapable of modifying "previous" states, though not incapable of modifying their recollection. Today's misadventure is no more real than yesterday's felicity. I will look for a more concrete example: At the beginning of August 1824, Captain Isidoro Suárez, at the head of a squadron of Peruvian hussars, decided the Victory of Junín; at the beginning of August 1824, De Quincey issued a diatribe against *Wilhelm Meisters Lehrjahre;* these deeds were not contemporaneous (they are now), inasmuch as the two men died—the one in the city of Montevideo, the other in Edinburgh—knowing nothing about each other. . . . Every instant is autonomous. Not vengeance nor pardon nor jails nor even oblivion can modify the invulnerable past. No less vain to my mind are hope and fear, for they always refer to future events, that is, to events which will not happen to us, who are the minute present. They tell me that the present, the "specious present" of the psychologists, lasts from between several seconds and the smallest fraction of a second: such is the length of the history of the universe. Or better, there is no such thing as "the life of a man," nor even "one night in his life." Each moment we live exists, not the imaginary combination of these moments. The universe, the sum total of all events, is a collection no less ideal than the sum of all the horses of which Shakespeare dreamt—one, many, none?—between 1592 and 1594. And: if time is a mental process, how can myriads of men, or even two distinct men, share it at all?

The argument set forth in the preceding paragraphs, rather encumbered and interrupted by examples, may seem intricate. I will find a more direct method. Let us consider a life in whose course repetitions abound: my life, for instance. I never pass in front of the Recoleta cemetery without remembering that my father, my grandparents, and great-grandparents are buried there, just as I shall be; then I remember having remembered the same thing innumerable times before; I can not walk through the outlying neighborhoods of the city in the silence of the night without thinking that nighttime is pleasing precisely because it does away with useless details, like memory; I can not lament the loss of a love or a friendship without meditating on how one only loses what one really never had; each time I cross one of the streets in South Buenos Aires, I think of you, Helen; every time the wind brings me the odor of eucalyptus, I think of Adrogué in my childhood; each time I recollect Fragment 91 of Heraclitus, *You never go down to the same stream twice,* I admire his dialectical skill, for the facility with which we accept the first meaning ("The stream is another") clandestinely imposes upon us the second meaning ("I am another") and grants us the illusion of having invented it; every time I hear a Germanophile running down Yiddish, I reflect that Yiddish is, after all, a German dialect, only slightly tainted by the language of the Holy Ghost. These tautologies (and others which I keep back) are my entire life. Naturally, they repeat themselves without precision; there are variations of emphasis, differences of temperature, of light, of general physiological condition. I suspect, nonetheless, that the number of circumstantial variations is not infinite: we can postulate, in the mind of an individual (or of two individuals who do not know each other but in both of whom the same process is operative), two identical moments. Once this identity is postulated, we may ask: Are not these identical moments the same moment? Is not *one single repeated terminal point* enough to break up and confound the series in time? Are not the fervent Shakespeareans who give themselves over to a line of Shakespeare, are they not, literally, Shakespeare?

I do not know, yet, the ethics of the system I have here outlined. I do not know if they exist. The fifth paragraph of the fourth chapter of the treatise *Sanhedrin* of the Mishnah declares that, as far as the Justice of God is concerned, whoever kills one man destroys the world. If there is no plurality, whoever would annihilate all mankind would be no more culpable than primitive and solitary Cain—an orthodox point of view—nor more universal in his destructiveness—which may be magical. That is the way I understand it, too. Clangorous general catastrophes—conflagrations, wars, epidemics—are a single grief, multiplied in numerous mirrors illusorily. Such is Bernard Shaw's judgment (*Guide to Socialism*, 86): "What you can suffer is the maximum that can be suffered on earth. If you die of starvation, you will suffer all the starvation there has been or will be. If ten thousand people die with you, their participation in your lot will not make you be ten thousand times more hungry nor multiply the time of your agony ten thousand times. Do not let yourself be overcome by the horrible sum of human sufferings; such a sum does not exist. Neither poverty nor pain are cumulative." (Cf. also *The Problem of Pain*, VII, by C. S. Lewis.)

Lucretius (*De rerum natura*, I, 830) attributes to Anaxagoras the doctrine that gold consists of particles of gold, fire of sparks, bone of tiny imperceptible bones. Josiah Royce, perhaps influenced by St. Augustine, is of the opinion that time is made up of time and that "every *now* within which something happens is therefore *also* a succession" (*The World and the Individual*, II, 139). That proposition is compatible with that of this essay.

II

All language is of a successive nature: it does not lend itself to reasoning on eternal, intemporal matters. Those of you who have followed the foregoing argumentation with no pleasure, may well prefer the following page written in 1928. I have mentioned it already, I mean the narrative titled *"Sentirse en muerte"*:

"I want to set down here an experience I had some nights ago, a trifling matter too evanescent and ecstatic to be called an adventure, too irrational and sentimental to be called a thought. It is a matter, rather, of a scene and of its word: a word already foresaid by me, but not experienced until then with total dedication. I go on, now, to tell the story, including the accidents of time and place which define it.

"I remember it thusly: The afternoon preceding that night, I was at Barracas, a locality not customarily visited by me and one whose distance from the places I later traversed lent an exotic savor to that day. The night had no destiny at all; since it was clear outside, I went out, after dinner, to walk and remember. I had no wish to take any determined route on that stroll; I attempted, rather, a maximum latitude of probabilities in order not to wear out expectation with an obligatory anticipation of a single one of them. I was able, within the imperfect limits of possibility, to walk, as they say, at random. I accepted, without any conscious prejudice but that of avoiding the wider avenues and streets, the most obscure invitations of chance. Still and all, a kind of familiar gravitation led me on, toward certain quarters, whose names I have every wish to remember always and which call forth reverence from my heart. I do not wish in this manner to signify my own quarter of the city, the precise compass of my own infancy, but rather its still-mysterious environs: confines I have altogether possessed in words and very little in reality, confines both neighboring and mythological. For me, those penultimate streets, almost as effectively unknown as the excavated foundations of our own house or our invisible skeleton, are the reverse of the familiar, the very back of the known. My walk brought me to a corner. I breathed the night in a serene holiday from thought. The vision before me, in no wise complicated, in any case, was simplified even further by my fatigue. The very fact that it was typical made it unreal. The street was one of low houses, and though its first sign was one of poverty, the second was certainly one of joyousness. It was of the poorest and the prettiest quality at once. No house ventured to press upon the street; the fig tree was dark over the corner wall; the outer doorways—higher than the lengthened outlines of the walls—seemed made of the same infinite substance as the night. The sidewalk was escarped over the street; the street was of elemental clay, clay of an as yet unconquered America. Further down, the narrow street became part of the pampa, dwindling into the Maldonado. Above the turbid and chaotic earth a rose-colored wall seemed, rather than to house the moonlight, to effuse an intimate light of its own. There could be no better name for tenderness than this rose color.

"I stood looking at this simple scene. I thought, out loud most probably: 'It's the same as it was thirty years ago. . . .' I thought back to that date: a recent enough time in other countries, but already a remote one in this fast-changing part of the world. Perhaps a bird was singing and I felt for it a small, close affection, a bird-size affection; but most probably there was no other sound in this vertiginous silence than the equally timeless sound of the crickets. The facile thought *I am in eighteen hundred and* . . . ceased being a set of approximate words and deepened into a reality. I felt dead, I felt myself an abstract perceiver of the world; I felt an indefinite fear imbued with science, the clearest metaphysics. I did not believe I had gone upstream on the presumed Waters of Time. No. Rather, I suspected I was in possession of the reticent or absent sense of the inconceivable word *eternity*. Only later did I succeed in defining this piece of imagination.

"Now, I write it down in this way: That pure representation of homogeneous events and matter—the clear night, the diaphanous wall, the provincial scent of honeysuckle, the elemental earth—is not merely identical to what was once represented at that corner so many years before, it is, without similarities or repetitions, the very same. If we can intuit that identity, time is a delusion. The indifference and inseparability of one moment in time's apparent yesterday from another moment in time's apparent today are enough to cause time's disintegration.

"It is evident that the number of such moments, human moments, is not infinite. The elemental ones—the moments of physical suffering and physical pleasure, the moments of sleep's approach, those of listening to a single piece of music, those of great intensity or great lassitude—are even more impersonal. I derive, in advance, the following conclusion: life is too poor not to be also immortal. But we do not even have the assurance of our own paucity, inasmuch as time, easily refutable by the senses, is not by the intellect, from whose essence the concept of succession seems inseparable. Thus, this half-glimpsed idea remains an anecdote of the emotions, and the true moment of ecstasy and the possible insinuation of eternity—which that night lavished on me—are confined, in confessed irresolution, to this sheet of paper."

B

Of the many doctrines recorded in the history of philosophy perhaps idealism is the oldest and most widespread. This observation belongs to Carlyle (*Novalis*, 1829); he alleges that among the philosophers whom it would be legitimate to include, without hope of ever completing the infinite roll, one might fittingly mention the Platonists, for whom the only realities are the archetypes (Norris, Judas, Abrabanel, Gemistus, Plotinus), the theologians, for whom everything that is not the divinity is contingent (Malebranche, Johannes Eckhart), the monists, who make the universe a vain adjective of the Absolute (Bradley, Hegel, Parmenides). . . . Idealism is as ancient as metaphysical disquiet. Its most acute apologist, George Berkeley, flourished in the eighteenth century: contrary to what Schopenhauer declared (*Die Welt als Wille und Vorstellung*, II, 1), his merit could not consist in the intuition of that doctrine but rather in the arguments he conceived in order to attest to it. Berkeley used those arguments against the notion of matter; Hume applied them to the mind; my purpose is to apply them to time. First I shall recapitulate the diverse stages of this dialectic.

Berkeley denied matter. This did not mean, of course, that he denied colors, odors, savors, sounds, and tactile sen-

sations; what he denied was that, aside from these perceptions, all of which make up the external world, there might
be something invisible, intangible, called matter. He denied
there could be pains no one felt, colors no one saw, forms
no one touched. He argued that to add matter to our perceptions is to add to the world another inconceivable and
superfluous world. He believed in the world of appearances
our senses weave for us, but he understood that the material world (Toland's, say) is an illusory duplication. He
observed (*Principles of Human Knowledge*, 3): "That neither our thoughts, nor passions, nor ideas formed by the
imagination, exist without the mind, is what everybody will
allow. And it seems no less evident that the various sensations or ideas imprinted on the sense, however blended or
combined together (that is, whatever objects they compose),
cannot exist otherwise than in a mind perceiving them. . . .
The table I write on I say exists—that is, I see and feel
it; and if I were out of my study I should say it existed—
meaning thereby that if I was in my study I might perceive
it, or that some other spirit actually does perceive it. . . .
For as to what is said of the absolute existence of unthinking things without any relation to their being perceived, that
seems perfectly unintelligible. Their *esse* is *percipi,* nor is it
possible they should have any existence out of the minds or
thinking things which perceive them."

In Paragraph 23 he added, foreseeing objections: "But,
say you, surely there is nothing easier than for me to imagine trees, for instance, in a park, or books existing in a
closet, and nobody by to perceive them. I answer, you may say
so, there is no difficulty in it; but what is all this, I beseech
you, more than framing in your mind certain ideas which
you call *books* and *trees,* and at the same time omitting to
frame the idea of any one that may perceive them? But do
not you yourself perceive or think of them all the while?
This therefore is nothing to the purpose; it only shews you

have the power of imagining or forming ideas in your mind: but it doth not shew that you can conceive it possible the objects of your thought may exist without the mind. . . ."

In Paragraph 6 he had already declared: "Some truths there are so near and obvious to the mind that a man need only open his eyes to see them. Such I take this important one to be, to wit, that all the choir of heaven and furniture of the earth, in a word all those bodies which compose the mighty frame of the world, have not any subsistence with- out a mind, that their *being* is to be perceived or known; that consequently so long as they are not actually perceived by me, or do not exist in my mind or that of any other created spirit, they must either have no existence at all, or else subsist in the mind of some Eternal Spirit. . . ." (Berke- ley's God is an ubiquitous spectator whose purpose is to lend coherence to the world.)

The doctrine I have just explained has been interpreted in perverse ways. Herbert Spencer believed he had refuted it (*Principles of Psychology,* VIII, 6), reasoning that if nothing exists outside consciousness, then consciousness must be infinite in time and space. The first is evident if we understand that all time is time perceived by someone, but erroneous if we infer that this time must necessarily embrace an infinite number of centuries; the second is il- licit, inasmuch as Berkeley repeatedly denied an absolute space (*Principles of Human Knowledge,* 116; *Siris,* 266). Even more indecipherable is the error into which Schopen- hauer fell (*Die Welt als Wille und Vorstellung,* II, 1) when he held that for the idealists the world is a phenomenon of the brain. Berkeley, however, had written (*Three Dialogues between Hylas and Philonous,* II): "The brain therefore you speak of, being a sensible thing, exists only in the mind. Now, I would fain know whether you think it reasonable to suppose, that one idea or thing existing in the mind, oc- casions all other ideas. And if you think so, pray how do you account for the origin of that primary idea or brain itself?" The brain, in truth, is no less a part of the external world than the constellation of the Centaur.

Berkeley denied that there was such a thing as an object behind our sense impressions; David Hume denied that there was such a thing as a subject behind our perception of change. The first denied matter, the second denied spirit; the first had not wanted us to add to the succession of impressions the metaphysical notion of matter, the second did not want us to add to the succession of mental states the metaphysical notion of an I. So logical is this extension of Berkeley's arguments, that Berkeley had already foreseen them (as Alexander Campbell Fraser noted) and went so far as to try to challenge it by means of the Cartesian *ergo sum*. "In consequence of your own principles, it should follow that you are only a system of floating ideas, without any substance to support them. Words are not to be used without a meaning. And as there is no more meaning in spiritual substance than in material substance, the one is to be exploded as well as the other." Thus reasons Hylas, anticipating Hume, in the third and last of Berkeley's *Three Dialogues between Hylas and Philonous*. Hume corroborates this idea (in *Treatise of Human Nature*, I, 4, 6): "We are a bundle or collection of different perceptions, which succeed each other with an inconceivable rapidity. . . . The mind is a kind of theatre, where several perceptions successively make their appearance; pass, re-pass, glide away, and mingle in an infinite variety of postures and situations. . . . The comparison of the theatre must not mislead us. They are the successive perceptions only, that constitute the mind; nor have we the most distant notion of the place, where these scenes are represented, or of the materials, of which it is compos'd."

Once the idealist argument is admitted, it is my understanding that it is possible—perhaps inevitable—to go further. For Berkeley, time is "the succession of ideas in my mind, which flows uniformly and is participated in by all beings" (*Principles of Human Knowledge*, 98); for Hume, it is "a succession of indivisible moments" (*Treatise of Human Nature*, I, 2, 3). However, with both matter and spirit—continuities—denied, with space denied, I do not know by what right we are to retain that continuity which is time. Outside each perception (real or conjectural) matter does not exist; outside each mental state spirit does not exist; neither then must time exist outside each present moment. Let us take a moment of the utmost simplicity: for example, the moment of Chuang Tzu's dream. (*Chuang Tzu*, Herbert Allen Giles, 1899.) Some twenty-four centuries ago, Chuang Tzu dreamt he was a butterfly, and, when he awoke he was not sure whether he was a man who had dreamt he was a butterfly or a butterfly who now dreamt he was a man. Let us not consider the moment of awakening, but the moment of the dream itself, or one of its moments. "I dreamt I was a butterfly fluttering through the air knowing nothing at all of Chuang Tzu," says the ancient text. We shall never know whether Chuang Tzu saw a garden over which he seemed to flutter or whether he saw a mobile yellow triangle, which was doubtless himself, but it is clear that the image was subjective, even though it was supplied to him by memory. The doctrine of psychophysical parallelism will hold that the image in question must have corresponded to some change in the dreamer's nervous system; according to Berkeley, at that moment the body of Chuang Tzu did not exist, nor did the black bedroom in which he was dreaming, save as a perception in the mind of God. Hume simplifies what happened even more. According to him, at that moment the spirit of Chuang Tzu did not exist; all that existed were the colors of the dream and the certainty of his being a butterfly. He existed as a momentary term in the "bundle or collection of different perceptions" which constituted, some four centuries before Christ, the mind of Chuang Tzu; he existed as the term *n* in an infinite temporal series, between *n* − 1 and *n* + 1. There is no other reality, for idealism, than that of mental processes; to add an objective butterfly to the butterfly one perceives seems, in its eyes, a vain duplication; to add an I to the mental processes seems, in its eyes, as no less exorbitant. Idealism holds that there was a dreaming, a perceiving, but not a dreamer nor even a dream; it holds that to speak of objects and subjects is to fall into an impure mythology. Now then, if each psychic state is self-sufficient, if to link it to some circumstance or to an I is an illicit and idle addition, with what right do we later assign it a place in time? Chuang Tzu dreamt he was a butterfly and during the course of that dream he was not Chuang Tzu but a butterfly. How, with space and self abolished, can we link those dreaming moments to his waking moments and the feudal epoch of Chinese history? All of which does not mean that we shall never know, even if only approximately, the date of that dream; I merely mean that the chronological establishing of an event, of any event in the world, is foreign to it and outside it. In China, the dream of Chuang Tzu is proverbial; let us imagine that one of the almost infinite number of Chuang Tzu's readers dreams he is a butterfly and then that he is Chuang Tzu. Let us imagine that, by a not impossible chance, this dream repeats, point by point, the dream of the master. Once this identity is postulated, we may well ask: Are not those coinciding moments identical? Is not *one single term repeated* enough to break down and confound the history of the world, to reveal that there is no such history?

The denial of time involves two negations: the negation of the succession of terms in a series, and the negation of the synchronism of terms in two series. In fact, if each term is absolute, its relations are reduced to the consciousness that those relations exist. One state precedes another if it knows it is anterior; a state of G is contemporaneous to a state of H if it knows it is contemporaneous. Contrary to what Schopenhauer* affirmed in his table of fundamental truths (*Die Welt als Wille und Vorstellung*, II, 4), each fraction of time does not simultaneously fill the whole of space: time is not ubiquitous. (Of course, at this point in the argument, space no longer exists.)

Meinong, in his theory of apprehension, admits of the apprehension of imaginary objects: the fourth dimension, let us say, or Condillac's sensitive statue, or Lotze's hypothetical animal, or the square root of minus one. If the reasons I have indicated are valid, then matter, the I, the external world, universal history, our lives, all belong to that nebulous sphere.

Moreover, the phrase *negation of time* is ambiguous. It can mean the eternity of Plato or of Boethius and also the dilemmas of Sextus Empiricus. This (*Adversus mathematicos*, XI, 197) denies the past, which already was, and the future, which is not yet, and argues that the present is either divisible or indivisible. It is not indivisible, for in that case it would have no beginning to link it to the past nor end to link it to the future, nor even a middle, for whatever has no beginning or end has no middle. Neither is it divisible, for in that case it would consist of a part that was and another that is not. *Ergo,* the present does not exist; and since the past and the future do not exist either, time does not exist. F. H. Bradley rediscovers and improves this perplexity: he observes (in *Appearance and Reality,* IV) that if the now is divisible into other nows, it is no less complicated than time; and that if it is indivisible, time is merely a relation between intemporal things. Such reasoning, obviously, denies the parts in order then to deny the whole; I reject the

---

* And, earlier, by Newton, who maintained: "Each particle of space is eternal, each indivisible moment of duration is everywhere." (*Principia*, III, 42.)

whole in order to exalt each one of the parts. I have arrived, via the dialectics of Berkeley and Hume, at Schopenhauer's dictum: "The form of the phenomenon of will . . . is really only the *present,* not the future nor the past. The latter are only in the conception, exist only in the connection of knowledge, so far as it follows the principle of sufficient reason. No man has ever lived in the past, and none will live in the future; the *present* alone is the form of all life, and is its sure possession which can never be taken from it. . . . We might compare time to a constantly revolving sphere; the half that was always sinking would be the past, that which was always rising would be the future; but the indivisible point at the top, where the tangent touches, would be the extensionless present. As the tangent does not revolve with the sphere, neither does the present, the point of contact of the object, the form of which is time, with the subject, which has no form, because it does not belong to the knowable, but is the condition of all that is knowable." (*Die Welt als Wille und Vorstellung,* I, 54.) A fifth-century Buddhist treatise, the *Visuddhimagga* (*The Path to Purity*), illustrates the same doctrine by means of the same figure: "Strictly speaking, the life of a living being . . . lasts only as long as that of a thought. Just as a chariot wheel in rolling touches earth at only one point . . . so lasts . . . the period of one thought" (Radhakrishnan: *Indian Philosophy,* I, 373). Other Buddhist texts say that the world is annihilated and revives six thousand five hundred million times a day and that every man is an illusion, dizzily wrought by a series of solitary and momentary men. "The man in the past, of the past moment," the *Path to Purity* advises us, "has lived, but he does not live, nor will he live; the man of a future moment will live, but he has not lived nor does he now live; the man of the present moment lives, but he has not lived nor will he live" (*op. cit.,* I, 407), a dictum we may compare with

Plutarch's (*De E apud Delphos,* 18): "Yesterday's man died in today's, today's dies in tomorrow's."

And yet, and yet . . . To deny temporal succession, to deny the self, to deny the astronomical universe, are measures of apparent despair and of secret consolation. Our destiny (in contrast to Swedenborg's hell and the hell of Tibetan mythology) is not frightful because it is unreal; it is frightful because it is irreversible and ironbound. Time is the substance of which I am made. Time is a river which sweeps me along, but I am the river; it is a tiger which mangles me, but I am the tiger; it is a fire which consumes me, but I am the fire. The world, unfortunately, is real; I, unfortunately, am Borges.

FOOTNOTE TO THE PROLOGUE

There is no exposition of Buddhism which does not mention the *Milinda Panha,* a second century work of apologetics; this work reports on a debate whose interlocutors are the King of Bactriana, Menander, and the monk Nagasena. The latter argues that just as the King's carriage is not the wheels nor the chassis nor the axle nor the pole nor the yoke, neither is man matter nor form nor impressions nor ideas nor instincts nor consciousness. He is not the combination of those parts nor does he exist outside them. . . . At the end of the several-days-long debate, Menander (Milinda) converts to the faith of the Buddha.

The *Milinda Panha* has been rendered into English by Rhys Davids (Oxford, 1890–1894).

> Freund, es ist auch genug. Im Fall du mehr willst lesen,
> So geh und werde selbst die Schrift und selmst das Wesen.

—Angelus Silesius,
Cherubinischer Wandersmann. VI, 263 (1675).

—*Translated by* ANTHONY KERRIGAN

LIMITS

There is a line of Verlaine I shall not recall again,
There is a nearby street forbidden to my step,
There is a mirror that has seen me for the last time,
There is a door I have shut until the end of the world.
Among the books in my library (I have them before me)
There are some I shall never reopen.
This summer I complete my fiftieth year:
Death reduces me incessantly.

—Translated by ANTHONY KERRIGAN

LIMITS

Of all those streets that wander to the west,
there must be one (I do not know which one)
which unawares I have walked down for a last
indifferent time, the pawn of that Someone

who fixes in advance the omnipotent laws,
tracing a secret and unyielding graph
of all the dreams, the forms, and the shadows
which thread and unthread the texture of this life.

If there is an end to everything, and an appraisal,
and a last time and nothing more and forgetfulness,
who then will point out which person, in this house,
to whom we have said, without knowing it, farewell?

Through the glass, already gray, the night
withdraws, and among the pile of volumes
throwing steep shadows on the table's gloom,
there must be one which we will never read.

There is, in the South, more than one worn gate
with its rough stone jugs and prickly pear
forbidden to my feet, as if it were
a lithograph or an old print.

For you, there is some door you are closing for ever,
and for you too, some mirror vainly waits.
The crossroads seem to you open and clear,
and yet are watched by a Janus with four heads.

There is among all of your memories one
which is irreparably lost and gone.
They will not see you going down to that fountain,
neither the white sun nor the yellow moon.

Your voice will never recover what was said once
in the Persian, the language of birds and roses,
when at your dying, before the light disperses,
you wish to utter unforgettable things.

And the ever-flowing Rhône, and the lake,
all that vast yesterday on which rests my present?
It will be as lost as Carthage was,
when the Latin scourged it out with fire and salt.

I imagine, in the dawn, I hear a worn
murmur of multitudes, faltering, fading away.
They are everything that has loved me and forgotten;
Space, Time and Borges now are leaving me.

—*Translated by* ALASTAIR REID

THE CIRCULAR RUINS

> And if he left off dreaming about you . . .
>
> —*Through the Looking Glass,* VI.

No one saw him disembark in the unanimous night. No one saw the bamboo canoe running aground on the sacred mud. But within a few days no one was unaware that the taciturn man had come from the South and that his home had been one of the infinity of hamlets which lie upstream, on the violent flank of the mountain, where the Zend language is uncontaminated by Greek, and where leprosy is infrequent. The certain fact is that the anonymous gray man kissed the mud, scaled the bank without pushing aside (probably without even feeling) the sharp-edged sedges lacerating his flesh, and dragged himself, bloody and sickened, up to the circular enclosure whose crown is a stone colt or tiger, formerly the color of fire and now the color of ash. This circular clearing is a temple, devoured by ancient conflagration, profaned by the malarial jungle, its god unhonored now of men. The stranger lay beneath a pedestal. He was awakened, much later, by the sun at its height. He was not astonished to find that his wounds had healed. He closed his pale eyes and slept, no longer from weakness of the flesh but from a determination of the will. He knew that this temple was the place required by his inflexible purpose; he knew that the incessant trees had not been able to choke the ruins of another such propitious temple down river, a temple whose gods also were burned and dead; he knew that his immediate obligation was to dream. The disconsolate shriek of a bird awoke him about midnight. The prints of bare feet, some figs, and a jug told him that the people of the region had reverently spied out his dreaming and solicited his protection or feared his magic. He felt the cold chill of fear, and sought in the dilapidated wall for a sepulchral niche where he concealed himself under some unfamiliar leaves.

The purpose which impelled him was not impossible though it was supernatural. He willed to dream a man. He wanted to dream him in minute totality and then impose him upon reality. He had spent the full resources of his soul on this magical project. If anyone had asked him his own name or about any feature of his former life, he would have been unable to answer. The shattered and deserted temple suited his ends, for it was a minimum part of the visible world, and the nearness of the peasants was also convenient, for they took it upon themselves to supply his frugal needs. The rice and fruits of the tribute were nourishment enough for his body, given over to the sole task of sleeping and dreaming.

At first his dreams were chaotic. A little later they were dialectical. The stranger dreamt he stood in the middle of a circular amphitheater which was in some measure the fired temple; clouds of taciturn students wearied the tiers; the faces of the last rows looked down from a distance of several centuries and from a stellar height, but their every feature was precise. The dreamer himself was delivering lectures on anatomy, cosmography, magic: the faces listened anxiously and strove to answer with understanding, as if they guessed the importance of that examination, which would redeem one of them from his insubstantial state and interpolate him into the real world. In dreams or in waking the man continually considered the replies of his phantoms; he did not let himself be deceived by the impostors; in certain paradoxes he sensed an expanding intelligence. He was seeking a soul worthy of participating in the universe.

At the end of nine or ten nights he realized, with a certain bitterness, that he could expect nothing from those students who accepted his teaching passively, but that he could of those who sometimes risked a reasonable contradiction. The former, though deserving of love and affection, could never rise to being individuals; the latter already existed to a somewhat greater degree. One afternoon (now even the afternoons were tributaries of the dream; now he stayed awake for only a couple of hours at daybreak) he dismissed the entire vast illusory student body for good and retained only one pupil. This pupil was a silent, sallow, sometimes obstinate boy, whose sharp features repeated those of his dreamer. The sudden elimination of his fellow students did not disconcert him for very long; his progress, at the end of a few private lessons, made his master marvel. And nevertheless, catastrophe came. One day the man emerged from sleep as from a viscous desert, stared about at the vain light of evening, which at first he took to be dawn, and realized he had not dreamt. All that night and all the next day the intolerable lucidity of insomnia broke over him in waves. He was impelled to explore the jungle, to wear himself out; he barely managed some quick snatches of feeble sleep amid the hemlock, shot through with fugitive visions of a rudimentary type: altogether unserviceable. He strove to assemble the student body, but he had scarcely uttered a few words of exhortation before the college blurred, was erased. Tears of wrath scalded his old eyes in his almost perpetual vigil.

He realized that the effort to model the inchoate and vertiginous stuff of which dreams are made is the most arduous task a man can undertake, though he get to the bottom of all the enigmas of a superior or inferior order: much more arduous than to weave a rope of sand or mint coins of the faceless wind. He realized that an initial failure was inevitable. He vowed to forget the enormous hallucination by which he had been led astray at first, and he sought out another approach. Before essaying it, he dedicated a month to replenishing the forces he had squandered in delirium. He abandoned all premeditation concerned with dreaming, and almost at once managed to sleep through a goodly part of the day. The few times he did dream during this period he took no notice of the dreams. He waited until the disk of the moon should be perfect before taking up his task again. Then, on the eve, he purified himself in the waters of the river, worshiped the planetary gods, pronounced the lawful syllables of a powerful name and went to sleep. Almost at once he dreamt of a beating heart.

He dreamt it active, warm, secret, the size of a closed fist, garnet-colored in the half-light of a human body that boasted as yet no sex or face. He dreamt this heart with meticulous love, for fourteen lucid nights. Each night he saw it more clearly. He never touched it, but limited himself to witnessing it, to observing it or perhaps rectifying it with a glance. He watched it, lived it, from far and from near and from many angles. On the fourteenth night he ran his index finger lightly along the pulmonary artery, and then over the entire heart, inside and out. The examination satisfied him. The next night, he deliberately did not dream. He then took up the heart again, invoked the name of a planet, and set about to envision another one of the principal organs. Before the year was up he had reached the skeleton, the eyelids. The most difficult task, perhaps, proved to be the numberless hairs. He dreamt a whole man, a fine lad, but one who could not stand nor talk nor open his eyes. Night after night he dreamt him asleep.

In the Gnostic cosmogonies, demiurges fashion a red Adam who never manages to get to his feet: as clumsy and equally as crude and elemental as this dust Adam was the dream Adam forged by the nights of the wizard. One afternoon, the man almost destroyed all his work, but then changed his mind. (It would have been better for him had he destroyed it.) Having expended all the votive offerings to the numina of the earth and the river, he threw himself at the feet of the effigy, which was perhaps a tiger or perhaps a colt, and implored its unknown help. That evening, at twilight, he dreamt of the statue. He dreamt it alive, tremulous: it was no atrocious bastard of a tiger and a colt, but both these vehement creatures at once and also a bull, a rose, a tempest. This multiple god revealed to him that its terrestrial name was Fire, that in this same circular temple (and in others like it) it once had been offered sacrifices and been the object of a cult, and that now it would magically animate the phantom dreamt by the wizard in such wise that all creatures—except Fire itself and the dreamer—would believe the phantom to be a man of flesh and blood. It directed that once the phantom was instructed in the rites, he be sent to the other broken temple, whose pyramids persisted down river, so that some voice might be raised in glorification in that deserted edifice. In the dream of the man who was dreaming, the dreamt man awoke.

The wizard carried out the directives given him. He dedicated a period of time (which amounted, in the end, to two years) to revealing the mysteries of the universe and the cult of Fire to his dream creature. In his intimate being, he suffered when he was apart from his creation. And so every day, under the pretext of pedagogical necessity, he protracted the hours devoted to dreaming. He also reworked the right shoulder, which was perhaps defective. At times, he had the uneasy impression that all this had happened before. . . . In general, though, his days were happy ones: as he closed his eyes he would think: *Now I shall be with my son.* Or, more infrequently: *The son I have engendered is waiting for me and will not exist if I do not go to him.*

Little by little he got his creature accustomed to reality. Once, he ordered him to plant a flag on a distant mountain top. The next day the flag was fluttering on the peak. He tried other analogous experiments, each one more audacious than the last. He came to realize, with a certain bitterness, that his son was ready—and perhaps impatient—to be born. That night he kissed his child for the first time, and sent him to the other temple, whose remains were whitening down river, many leagues across impassable jungle and swamp. But first, so that his son should never know he was a phantom and should think himself a man like other men, he imbued him with total forgetfulness of his apprentice years.

His triumph and his respite were sapped by tedium. In the twilight hours of dusk or dawn he would prostrate himself before the stone figure, imagining his unreal child practicing identical rites in other circular ruins downstream. At night he did not dream, or dreamt as other men do. The sounds and forms of the universe reached him wanly, pallidly: his absent son was being sustained on the diminution of the wizard's soul. His life's purpose had been achieved; the man lived on in a kind of ecstasy. After a time—which some narrators of his story prefer to compute in years and others in lustra—he was awakened one midnight by two boatmen: he could not see their faces, but they told him of a magical man at a temple in the North, who walked on fire and was not burned. The wizard suddenly recalled the words of the god. He remembered that of all the creatures composing the world, only Fire knew his son was a phantom. This recollection, comforting at first, ended by tormenting him. He feared lest his son meditate on his abnormal privilege and somehow discover his condition of mere simulacrum. Not to be a man, to be the projection of another man's dream—what incomparable humiliation, what vertigo! Every father is concerned with the children he has procreated (which he has permitted) in mere confusion or felicity: it was only natural that the

wizard should fear for the future of his son, thought out
entrail by entrail and feature by feature on a thousand
and one secret nights.

The end of his caviling was abrupt, but not without fore-
warnings. First (after a long drought) a remote cloud, light
as a bird, appeared over a hill. Then, toward the South,
the sky turned the rosy color of a leopard's gums. Smoke
began to rust the metallic nights. And then came the panic
flight of the animals. And the events of several centuries
before were repeated. The ruins of the fire god's sanctuary
were destroyed by fire. One birdless dawn the wizard
watched the concentric conflagration close around the walls:
for one instant he thought of taking refuge in the river,
but then he understood that death was coming to crown
his old age and to absolve him of further work. He walked
against the florid banners of the fire. And the fire did not
bite his flesh but caressed and engulfed him without heat
or combustion. With relief, with humiliation, with terror,
he understood that he, too, was all appearance, that someone else was dreaming him.

—*Translated by* ANTHONY KERRIGAN

CHESS

I

In their serious corner, the players
move the gradual pieces. The board
detains them until dawn in its hard
compass: the hatred of two colors.

In the game, the forms give off a severe
magic: Homeric castle, gay
knight, warlike queen, king solitary,
oblique bishop, and pawns at war.

Finally, when the players have gone in,
and when time has eventually consumed them,
surely the rites then will not be done.

In the east, this war has taken fire.
Today, the whole earth is its provenance.
Like that other, this game is for ever.

II

Tenuous king, slant bishop, bitter queen,
straightforward castle and the crafty pawn—
over the checkered black and white terrain
they seek out and enjoin their armed campaign.

They do not realize the dominant
hand of the player rules their destiny.
They do not know an adamantine fate
governs their choices and controls their journey.

The player, too, is captive of caprice
(the sentence is Omar's) on another ground
crisscrossed with black nights and white days.

God moves the player, he, in turn, the piece.
But what god beyond God begins the round
of dust and time and dream and agonies?

—*Translated by* ALASTAIR REID

THE GOLEM

If (as the Greek asserts in the *Cratylus*)
The name is archetype to the thing,
The rose is in the letters of "rose"
And the length of the Nile in "Nile."

Thus, compounded of consonants and vowels,
There must be a terrible Name, which essence
Ciphers as God and Omnipotence
Preserves in consummate letters and syllables.

Adam, and the stars, knew it
In the Garden. The iron rust of sin
(Say the cabalists) has effaced it
And the generations have lost the word.

The artifices and candor of man
Are endless. We know that there came a day
On which the People of God sought the Name
In the vigils of the ghetto:

The memory is still green and vivid—
Not in the manner of other memories like
Vague shadows insinuated in a vague history—
Of Judah Lion, rabbi of Prague.

Burning to know what God knew,
Judah Lion gave himself up to permutations
Of letters and complex variations:
And at length pronounced the Name which is the Key,

The Portal, the Echo, the Host, the Palace,
Over a doll which, with torpid hands,
He wrought to teach the arcana
Of Letters, Time, and Space.

The simulacrum raised its heavy
Lids and saw forms and colors
It did not understand, lost in a din,
And attempted fearsome movements.

Gradually it saw itself (even as we)
Imprisoned in that sonorous net
Of Before, After, Yesterday, While, Now,
Left, Right, I, Thou, Those, Others.

(The cabalist who officiated as divinity
Called his farfetched creature "Golem":
These truths are related by Scholem
In a learned passage of his volume.)

The rabbi explained the universe to him
(*This is my foot; this is yours; this, the rope*)
And, after many years, taught the aberration
To sweep the synagogue, as best he might.

There must have been some error in graphics
Or in articulating the Sacred Name:
For despite the most bizarre wizardry
The apprentice man never learned to talk.

Its eyes—less a man's than a dog's,
And even less a dog's than a thing's—
Would follow the rabbi through the equivocal
Twilight of the dim unworldly retreat.

There was something too untoward in the Golem
For at his approach the rabbi's cat
Would hide. (This cat does not appear in Scholem
But I intuit it across all these years.)

Raising its filial hands to God
It copied the devotions of its god
Or, stupefied and smirking, it would bend
Into the concave salaams of the Orient.

The rabbi gazed fondly on his creature
And with some terror. *How* (he asked himself)
Could I have engendered this grievous son,
And left off inaction, which is wisdom?

Why did I decide to add to the infinite
Series one more symbol? Why, to the vain
Skein which unwinds in eternity
Did I add another cause, effect, and woe?

At the hour of anguish and vague light
He would rest his eyes on his Golem.
Who can tell us what God felt,
As He gazed on His rabbi in Prague?

—*Translated by* ANTHONY KERRIGAN

INFERNO I, 32

In the final years of the twelfth century, from twilight of dawn to twilight of dusk, a leopard looked upon some wooden planks, some vertical iron bars, men and women who were always different, a thick wall and, perhaps, a stone trough filled with dry leaves. The leopard did not know, could not know, that what he craved was love and cruelty and the hot pleasure of rending and the odor of a deer on the wind; and yet something within the animal choked him and something rebelled, and God spoke to him in a dream: *You live and will die in this prison, so that a man I know may look at you a certain number of times and not forget you and put your figure and your symbol in a poem which has its precise place in the scheme of the universe. You suffer captivity, but you will have furnished a word to the poem.* In the dream, God enlightened the rough beast, so that the leopard understood God's reasons and accepted his destiny; and yet, when he awoke, he felt merely an obscure resignation, a gallant ignorance, for the machinery of the world is overly complex for the simplicity of a wild beast.

Years later, Dante lay dying in Ravenna, as little justified and as much alone as any other man. In a dream, God revealed to him the secret purpose of his life and labor; in wonderment, Dante knew at last who he was and what he was and he blessed his bitter days. Tradition holds that on awakening he felt he had received and then lost something infinite, something he could not recuperate, or even glimpse, for the machinery of the world is overly complex for the simplicity of men.

—*Translated by* ANTHONY KERRIGAN

THE OTHER TIGER

And the craft createth a semblance.

—Morris, *Sigurd the Volsung* (1876).

I think of a tiger. The half-light enhances
the vast and painstaking library
and seems to set the bookshelves at a distance;
strong, innocent, new-made, bloodstained,
it will move through its jungle and its morning,
and leave its track across the muddy
edge of a river, unknown, nameless
(in its world, there are no names, nor past, nor future
only the sureness of the passing moment)
and it will cross the wilderness of distance
and sniff out in the woven labyrinth
of smells the smell peculiar to morning
and the scent of deer, delectable.
Among the slivers of bamboo, I notice
its stripes, and I have an inkling of the skeleton
under the magnificence of the skin, which quivers.
In vain, the convex oceans and the deserts
spread themselves across the earth between us;
from this one house in a remote lost seaport
in South America, I dream you, follow you,
oh tiger on the fringes of the Ganges.

Afternoon creeps in my spirit and I keep thinking
that the tiger I am conjuring in my poem
is a tiger made of symbols and of shadows,
a sequence of prosodic measures,
scraps remembered from encyclopedias,
and not the deadly tiger, the luckless jewel
which in the sun or the deceptive moonlight

follows its paths, in Bengal or Sumatra,
of love, of indolence, of dying.
Against the symbolic tiger, I have planted
the real one, it whose blood runs hotly,
and today, 1959, the third of August,
a slow shadow spreads across the prairie,
but still, the act of naming it, of guessing
what is its nature and its circumstances
creates a fiction, not a living creature,
not one of those who wander on the earth.

Let us look for a third tiger. This one
will be a form in my dream like all the others,
a system and arrangement of human language,
and not the tiger of the vertebrae
which, out of reach of all mythology,
paces the earth. I know all this, but something
drives me to this ancient and vague adventure,
unreasonable, and still I keep on looking
throughout the afternoon for the other tiger,
the other tiger which is not in this poem.

—*Translated by* ALASTAIR REID

A YELLOW ROSE

The illustrious Giambattista Marino, whom the unanimous mouths of Fame—to use an image dear to him—proclaimed the new Homer and the new Dante, did not die that afternoon or the next. And yet, the immutable and tacit event that happened then was in effect the last event of his life. Laden with years and glory, the man lay dying in a vast Spanish bed with carved bedposts. It takes no effort to imagine a lordly balcony, facing west, a few steps away, and, further down, the sight of marble and laurels and a garden whose stone steps are duplicated in a rectangle of water. A woman has placed a yellow rose in a vase. The man murmurs the inevitable verses which—to tell the truth—have begun to weary him a little:

> *Blood of the garden, pomp of the walk,*
> *gem of spring, April's eye . . .*

Then came the revelation. Marino *saw* the rose as Adam might have seen it in Paradise. And he sensed that it existed in its eternity and not in his words, and that we may make mention or allusion of a thing but never express it at all; and that the tall proud tomes that cast a golden penumbra in an angle of the drawing room were not—as he had dreamed in his vanity—a mirror of the world, but simply one more thing added to the universe.

This illumination came to Marino on the eve of his death, and, perhaps, it had come to Homer and Dante too.

—Translated by ANTHONY KERRIGAN

BALTASAR GRACIÁN

Labyrinths, quibbles, emblems,
Such bleak laborious minutiae
Were all this Jesuit knew of poetry,
Which he had reduced to stratagems.

No music in his soul; but this inane
Herbarium of metaphors and punning
And a veneration of cunning
And contempt for the human and superhuman.

Homer's ancient voice he never heard,
Or the voice—silver and moonlight—of Virgil;
Nor saw Oedipus the accursed in exile
Nor Christ who is dying on a piece of board.

The stars, the radiant eastern stars
That in the vast aurora slowly fade,
Of these he blasphemously said
Chickens of the celestial acres.

As ignorant of divine love he was
As of that other burning in the bone;
The Pale One surprised him one afternoon
As he was reading El Marino's stanzas.

His later destiny is not given;
The dust that yesterday was his frame
Loosed to the changes of the tainted grave,
The soul of Gracián rose up to heaven.

What did he feel then contemplating plainly
The Archetypes and the Splendors?
Perhaps he cried and told himself: Vainly
I sought nourishment in shadows and errors.

What happened when the relentless
Sun of God, The Truth, put forth its fire?
Maybe the light of God left him blind there
In the center of the endless heavens.

I know another ending. Doped on his themes
Infinitesimal, Gracián never noticed heaven
And turns over in his memory as ever
Labyrinths, quibbles, and emblems.

—*Translated by* IRVING FELDMAN

TO AN OLD POET*

You wander over the plains of Castile
and you barely see them. An obscure
passage from St. John is your care
and you scarcely pause in the yellow

sunset. The vagrant light gives off
madness, and at the distant eastern end
that mocking scarlet moon distends
and is perhaps the mirror of the Wrath.

You lift your eyes to look at it. Now,
a memory of something starts up and goes out
that once was yours. You bow

your pallid head and sadly wander on,
not remembering the line that once you wrote:
and his epitaph the blood-stained moon.

—*Translated by* JILL JARRELL

---

* Francisco de Quevedo, 1580–1645, wrote, some time after the death
of his patron, the Duke of Osuna, a celebration of his memory, one line
of which reads: *Y su epitafio la sangrienta luna,* the last line of the
Borges poem.—*Editor's note.*

PARABLE OF THE PALACE

That day, the Yellow Emperor showed the poet through his palace. As they moved on, they left behind them, one after another, the first western terraces that, like gradins of an almost boundless amphitheater, slope toward a garden whose metal mirrors and intricate juniper borders prefigured the labyrinth. They lost themselves in it, gaily at first, as if consenting to a game and later not without misgivings, for its straight avenues underwent a very slight but continuous curvature and secretly were circles. Toward midnight their observation of the planets and the opportune sacrifice of a turtle enabled them to extricate themselves from that seemingly bewitched region, but they did not free themselves from the feeling of being lost, which accompanied them until the end. Afterward they passed through antechambers and patios and libraries and a hexagonal drawing room with a water clock, and one morning they made out from a tower a man of stone, later lost to them forever. In sandalwood canoes, they crossed many glittering rivers, or a single river many times. The imperial retinue would pass by and the people would prostrate themselves; but one day they arrived at an island in which someone did not do so, because he had never seen the Son of Heaven, and the executioner had to behead him. Their eyes looked with indifference on black-haired heads and black dances and complicated gold masks; what was real would confound itself with what was dreamt or, rather, the real was one of the configurations of the dream. It seemed impossible that the earth should be anything other than gardens, watercourses, architectural and other forms of splendor. Each hundred steps a tower cut the air; to the eye their color was identical, though the first one was yellow and the last scarlet, so delicate were the gradations and so long the series.

It was at the foot of the penultimate tower that the poet (who had seemed remote from the wonders that were a marvel to all) recited the brief composition that today we link indissolubly to his name and that, as the most elegant historians repeat, presented him with immortality and death. The text has been lost; there are those who believe that it consisted of a line of verse; others, of a single word. What is certain, and incredible, is that all the enormous palace was, in its most minute details, there in the poem, with each illustrious porcelain and each design on each porcelain and the penumbrae and the light of each dawn and twilight, and each unfortunate or happy instant in the glorious dynasties of mortals, of gods and of dragons that had inhabited it from the unfathomable past. Everyone was silent, but the Emperor exclaimed: *You have robbed me of my palace!* And the executioner's iron sword cut the poet down.

Others tell the story differently. There cannot be any two things alike in the world; the poet had only to recite the poem, they say, when the palace disappeared, as though abolished and obliterated by the last syllable. Such legends are, to be sure, no more than literary fictions. The poet was the emperor's slave and died as such; his composition fell into oblivion because it merited oblivion and his descendants still seek, and will not find, the word for the universe.

—*Translated by* CARMEN FELDMAN ALVAREZ DEL OLMO

THE WALL AND
THE BOOKS

He, whose long wall the wand'ring Tartar bounds . . .
—*Dunciad*, II, 76.

I read, a few days ago, that the man who ordered the almost infinite wall of China to be built was that First Emperor, Shih Huang Ti, who likewise ordered all books antedating him to be burned. That these two vast undertakings—the five or six hundred leagues of stone thrown up against the barbarians, and the rigorous abolition of history, that is, of the past—should originate with the same person and be in some way his attributes, inexplicably pleased and, at the same time, disturbed me. The purpose of this note is to examine the reasons for that emotion.

Historically speaking, there is no mystery about the two measures. Contemporaneous with the wars of Hannibal, Shih Huang Ti, the king of Tsin, took control of the Six Kingdoms and wiped out their feudal system; he built the wall because walls were defenses; he burned the books because the opposition invoked them in order to praise the ancient emperors. Burning books and building fortifications are occupations common among princes; what was singular in the case of Shih Huang Ti was the scale on which he operated. This is what we are given to understand by certain Sinologists; I feel, however, that the facts I have related are something more than an exaggeration or a hyperbole for relatively trivial acts. Walling off an orchard or a garden is common enough, but not walling off an empire. Again, it is no trifle to require the most traditional of races to renounce its memory of the past, whether mythical or real. The Chinese had a recorded history of 3000 years (which included, during those years, the Yellow Emperor and Chuang Tzu and Confucius and Lao Tzu) when Shih Huang Ti ordered that history begin with him.

Shih Huang Ti had exiled his mother for being a libertine; the orthodox found this stern justice to be entirely impious; perhaps Shih Huang Ti wished to wipe out the canonical books because they accused him; perhaps Shih Huang Ti wished to abolish the whole of the past because he wished to abolish a single memory: that of his mother's disgrace. (In the same way, a king, in Judea, killed all the children in order to kill one child.) This conjecture merits attention, but it tells us nothing of the wall, the myth's second facet. Shih Huang Ti, according to historians, forbade the mention of death and searched for the elixir of immortality and shut himself up in a symbolic palace that had as many rooms as there are days in the year; this suggests that the wall in space and the conflagration in time were magical barriers designed to hold back death. Baruch Spinoza has written that all things desire to persist in their being; perhaps the Emperor and his wizards believed immortality to be inherent and that corruption cannot enter a closed circle. Perhaps the Emperor wanted to re-create the beginning of time and called himself the First in order to be indeed first and named himself Huang Ti in order to somehow be Huang Ti, that legendary emperor who invented writing and the compass. The latter, according to the Book of Rites, gave things their true names; similarly, Shih Huang Ti boasted, on inscriptions that still endure, that during his dominion each thing would have the name befitting it. He dreamed of founding an immortal dynasty and commanded his heirs to call themselves Second Emperor, Third Emperor, Fourth Emperor, and so on to infinity. . . . I have spoken of a magical intention. It may also be supposed that the erection of the wall and the burning of the books were not simultaneous acts. This would, according to the order we preferred, give us the image of a king who began by destroying but then resigned himself to preserving, or of a disillusioned king who undertook to destroy what he had previously defended. Both conjectures are dramatic, but are, so far as I know, without historical foundation. Herbert Allen Giles tells us that those guilty of concealing books were branded with a red-hot iron and condemned to work for the rest of their lives on the monstrous wall. This item favors or at least admits of another interpretation. Perhaps the wall was a metaphor and Shih Huang Ti condemned those who adored the past to a task as vast, as stupid, and as useless as the past itself. Perhaps the wall was a challenge and Shih Huang Ti thought: "Men love the past, and I and my executioners are helpless against that love, but some day there will be a man who feels as I do, and he will destroy my wall as I have destroyed the books, and he will obliterate my memory and will be my shadow and my mirror and will not know it." Perhaps Shih Huang Ti walled in the empire because he knew it to be perishable and destroyed the books because they were sacred books, books that teach what the entire universe or the conscience of each man teaches. Perhaps the burning of the libraries and the construction of the wall are undertakings that secretly cancel themselves.

The firm wall, which at this and in every moment casts its system of shadows over lands I shall never see, is the shadow of a Caesar who ordered the most reverent of nations to burn its past; it is likely that, aside from the conjectures it permits, this idea itself moves us. (Its virtue may reside in its opposition, on an enormous scale, between constructing and destroying.) Generalizing upon this, we might infer that *all* forms possess their virtue in themselves and not in any conjectural "content." This would accord with Benedetto Croce's thesis; and Pater had already, in

1877, asserted that all the arts aspire to the condition of music, which is pure form. Music, states of happiness, mythology, faces scored by time, certain twilights, certain places, all want to tell us something, or told us something we should not have missed, or are about to tell us something. This imminence of a revelation that does not take place is, perhaps, the esthetic fact.

—*Translated by* IRVING FELDMAN

THE ENIGMA OF EDWARD FITZGERALD

A man, Umar ben Ibrahim, is born in Persia in the eleventh
century of the Christian era (for him, the fifth century of
the Mohammedan Hegira), and learns the Koran and Tradition from Hassan ben Sabbah, future founder of the sect
of Hashishin or Assassins, and from Nizam ul-Mulk, who
is to become vizier of Alp Arslan, and conquerer of the
Caucasus. Half-seriously, half in jest, the three friends
swear that if some day good fortune favors one of them,
the lucky one will not forget the others. In his crowning
years, Nizam achieves the rank of vizier. Umar asks him
for nothing more than a corner in the shade of his good
fortune from which to pray for the well-being of his friend
and to meditate on mathematics. (Hassan asks for and ob-
tains a high post and, at last, has the vizier stabbed to
death.) Umar receives from the treasury of Nishapur an
annual pension of ten thousand dinars and is able to devote
himself to his studies. He forswears astrology, but takes up
astronomy, collaborating in the reform of the calendar
sponsored by the sultan and composing a famous treatise
on algebra which provides numerical solutions for equations
of the first and second degree, and geometrical solutions,
by means of intersecting cones, for those of the third. The
mysteries of number and the stars do not exhaust his attention; he reads, in the solitude of his library, the texts
of Plotinus, who, in the vocabulary of Islam, is the Egyptian Plato or the Greek Master, and the fifty-odd epistles
of the heretical and mystical Encyclopedia of the Brothers
of Purity, in which it is reasoned that the universe is an
emanation of Unity, and will return to Unity. . . . He is

regarded as a proselyte of Alfarabi, who believed that
universal forms do not exist apart from things, and of
Avicenna, who taught that the world is everlasting. One
account of him informs us that he believes, or makes a
show of believing, in the transmigrations of the soul, from
human to animal body, and on one occasion spoke with an
ass, as Pythagoras spoke with a dog. He is an atheist, but is
well able to interpret in the orthodox manner the most
exacting passages of the Koran, since every cultured man
is a theologian, and since, in order to be one, faith is not
indispensable. In the intervals between astronomy, algebra,
and apologetics, Umar ben Ibrahim al-Khayyami works on
verse compositions of four lines, of which the first, the
second, and the last are rhymed; the most extensive manuscript attributes to him five hundred of these quatrains, a
number scant enough to do disservice to his fame, since in
Persia (as in the Spain of Lope and Calderón), the poet
must be prolific. In the year 517 of the Hegira, Umar is
reading a treatise entitled *The One and the Many*; a malaise or a premonition interrupts him. He gets up, marks
the page which his eyes will not see again, and makes his
peace with God, with that God which may or may not exist
and whose favor he has asked for in the difficult pages of
his algebra. He dies that same day, at the hour of the setting of the sun. Around that time, on an occidental island to
the north, unknown to the cartographers of Islam, a Saxon
king who has defeated a king of Norway is defeated by a
Norman duke.

Seven centuries flow past, with their lusters, their agonies
and their mutations; and in England, a man, FitzGerald, is
born, less of an intellect than Umar, but perhaps more sensitive, more wistful. FitzGerald is aware that literature is
his true destiny, and pursues it with indolence and tenacity.
Over and over again he reads *Don Quixote,* which seems to
him almost the greatest of books (he does not wish to be
unjust to Shakespeare and "dear old Virgil") and his pas-

sion embraces the dictionary in which he looks up words. He realizes that every man who has some music in his soul can make verses ten or a dozen times in his life if the stars are propitious, but he does not propose to abuse this modest gift. He is the friend of famous people (Tennyson, Carlyle, Dickens, Thackeray), and feels himself in no way inferior to them, despite his modesty and courtesy. He has published a gracefully written dialogue, *Euphranor,* and indifferent versions of Calderón and the great Greek tragedies. From the study of Spanish, he has gone on to Persian, and has begun a translation of *Mantiq al-Tayr,* that mystical epic about the birds who search for their king, Simurg, and finally arrive at his palace, which is across the seven seas, to discover that they are Simurg and that Simurg is each and every one of them. Around 1854, he is lent a manuscript collection of Umar's compositions, the verses put together with no other organization than the alphabetical order of their rhymes; FitzGerald puts some of them into Latin, and glimpses the possibility of turning them into a continuous, organically coherent book, beginning with the images of morning, the rose and the nightingale, and ending with those of night and the tomb. To this improbable and farfetched end, FitzGerald dedicates his life, that of an indolent, solitary, and monomaniacal man. In 1859, he publishes a first version of the *Rubáiyát,* which is followed by others, rich in variations and refinements. A miracle happens: from the lucky conjunction of a Persian astronomer who ventures into poetry and an English eccentric who explores Spanish and Oriental texts, without understanding them entirely, emerges an extraordinary poet who resembles neither of them. Swinburne writes that FitzGerald "has given to Omar Khayyám a permanent place among the major English poets," and Chesterton, aware of the mixture of romanticism and classicism in this extraordinary work, observes that it possesses at the same time "an elusive melody and a lasting message." Some critics take Fitz-

Gerald's *Omar* as an English poem with Persian allusions; FitzGerald interpolated, refined and invented, but his *Rubáiyát* seems, to us readers, to be both ancient and Persian.

The case calls for conjecture of a metaphysical nature. Umar, as we know, professed the Platonic and Pythagorean doctrine of the transition of the soul through many incarnations; with the passing of the centuries, his soul possibly found its reincarnation in England to fulfill, in a remote Germanic language with Latin overtones, the literary destiny that in Nishapur had been pushed aside by mathematics. Isaac Luria the Lion demonstrated that the soul of a dead man can enter the lost spirit of another to maintain or instruct him. Perhaps the spirit of Umar lodged, around 1857, in FitzGerald's. In the *Rubáiyát,* we read that the history of the universe is a spectacle which God conceives, stages, and then contemplates; this speculation (the technical name for it is pantheism) would permit us to believe that the Englishman could have re-created the Persian, since both were, in essence, God, or momentary faces of God.

More probable, and no less marvelous than these almost supernatural conjectures, is the assumption of a benevolent destiny. At times, the clouds take the shape of mountains or lions; by analogy, the wistfulness of Edward FitzGerald, and a manuscript on yellowing paper, in purple characters, forgotten in a vault of the Bodleian Library in Oxford, assume, for the good of us all, the shape of the poem.

Any collaboration is mysterious. This one, of an Englishman and a Persian, was more so than any other, because the two were very different, and in life might not have achieved friendship; it was death and vicissitude and time that brought it about that one should know of the other and both become a single poet.

—*Translated by* Alastair Reid

ARIOSTO AND THE ARABS

No one can write a book. Since
Before a book can really be
It needs the dawn, the dusk, centuries,
Arms, and the binding and sundering sea.

Ariosto thought as much, but dreamt
Again the dreams that had been dreamt
In the leisured pace of placid walks
Between dark pines and marble blocks.

The air of Italy was dense with dreams
Dreamed out of memory and oblivion
In the forms of far-off battles
Wearying the land in centuries of wars.

A legion lost in the deep valleys
Of Aquitania fell into an ambuscade:
And thus was born the dream of the sword
And the horn sounding at Roncevaux.

The dour Saxon drove his arms
And idols across the fields of England
In close unwieldy warfare
And left behind a dream named Arthur.

From the boreal islands where a blinded sun
Blurs the sea came another dream:
Of a sleeping virgin awaiting her lord
Within a charmed ring of fire.

From Persia or Parnassus came
The dream of the winged horse
Ridden hard by the armed enchanter
To disappear behind the desert sunset.

Ariosto saw the kingdoms of the earth
As from the back of this hippogriff:
An earth furrowed with the feasts of war
And the youthful love of the adventurer.

He saw in the world a garden dilate
—Behind a soft gold fog—
Its confines to include a more intimate garden
Where the love of Angelica and Medoro grew.

In *Orlando Furioso* a succession of loves
As disordered as bits of a kaleidoscope
Recall the illusory splendor
Opium allows Cathay.

He was as much at home with love
As with sweet irony, and dreamt
Thus modestly the singular castle
As altogether false as life.

As it does to all poets, Fortune
Or Destiny allotted him a rare lot:
He walked along Ferrara roads
And at the same time trod the moon.

Dross of dreams, shapeless muck
Left behind by the Nile of sleep:
But dreams it was which wove the skein
Of that illuminated labyrinth:

An enormous diamond in which a man
May lose himself most fortunately
Through ambits of indolent music
Beyond the scope of his flesh and name.

The whole of Europe got lost.
That maliciously ingenious art
Made possible Milton's weeping the end
Of Brandimarte and Dalinda's fall.

Europe was lost. But the vast dream
Gave compensation to the fame-filled folk
Inhabiting the Orient deserts
And the lion-haunted night.

The delightful book still dear
To time tells us of the king
Who, at daybreak, gave his queen
Of a night to the implacable scimitar.

Of wings that are stark night:
Cruel talons clutching an elephant:
Magnetic mountains whose embrace
Shatters ships to pieces:

The earth held up by a bull:
The bull by a fish: abracadabra,
Talismans and mystic words
That open gold caves in the granite.

Thus the Saracens dreamed
As they followed the flags of Agramante:
And this dream dreamed by veiled faces
In turbans took possession of the Occident.

Orlando is now a risible place
Of dilated uninhabited leagues
Of innocent but idle marvels:
A dream that no one now will dream

Shrunk by Islamic arts
To mere erudition, mere history,
It is left alone to dream itself.
(Glory is one of the forms of oblivion.)

Through the window the uncertain light,
Fading now, of one more afternoon
Falls upon the book, and again
Its gilt glows and is consumed.

In the empty room the silent book
Travels into time, and leaves behind
The hours of dawn and the hours of dusk
And my life, that hasty dream.

—*Translated by* ANTHONY KERRIGAN

AVERROËS' SEARCH

S'imaginant que la tragédie
n'est autre que l'art de louer . . .

—Ernest Renan, *Averroës,* 48 (1861).

Abu-al-Walīd Muhammad ibn-Ahmad ibn-Rushd (a century would be needed for this lengthy name to become simply Averroës, after first becoming Benraist and then Avenryz and even Aben-Rassad and Filius Rosadis) was busy redacting the eleventh chapter of the *Tahāfut al Tahāfut* ("The Incoherence of Incoherence"), in which he maintains, against the opinion of the Persian ascetic al-Ghazzāli, author of the *Tahāfut al Falasifa* ("The Incoherence of Philosophers"), that the Divinity knows only the general laws of the universe, those concerning the species, not those relating to the individual. He wrote with slow assurance, from right to left; the task of composing syllogisms and of linking up vast paragraphs did not prevent him from feeling, as if it were a sense of well-being, the cool deep house around him. In the depths of the siesta hour, amorous doves cooed huskily; from some invisible patio arose the murmur of a fountain; something in the blood of Averroës, whose ancestors came from Arabian deserts, was grateful for the constancy of water. Down below lay the gardens, the orchard; down below, the bustling Guadalquivir, and beyond, the beloved city of Córdoba, no less illustrious than Baghdad or Cairo, like a complex and delicate instrument; and all around (Averroës heard and felt it, too), the land of Spain stretched out to the border, the land of Spain, where there are few things, but where each one seems to exist in a substantive and eternal way.

His pen raced across the page, his proofs, irrefutable,

101

interwove themselves; but a slight preoccupation dimmed Averroës' felicity. It was not the fault of the *Tahāfut,* a fortuitous piece of work, but was caused by a problem of a philological nature, relating to the monumental work which would justify him in the eyes of mankind: his commentary on Aristotle. Fountainhead of all wisdom, the Greek had been given to the world to teach men all they might know. Averroës' lofty purpose was to interpret his books in the way that the ulema interpret the Koran. History records few acts more beautiful and more pathetic than this Arabic physician's consecration to the thoughts of a man from whom he was separated by fourteen centuries. To the intrinsic difficulties we should add the fact that Averroës, who had no knowledge of Syriac or Greek, was working on the translation of a translation. On the previous evening he had been nonplussed by two equivocal words at the beginning of the *Poetics*: the words *tragedy* and *comedy.* He had encountered them years before in the third book of the *Rhetoric.* No one within the compass of Islam intuited what they meant. Averroës had exhausted the pages of Alexander of Aphrodisia in vain; vainly he had collated the versions of the Nestorian philosopher Hunain ibn-Ishaq and of abu-Bashar Mata. The two arcane words pullulated in the text of the *Poetics;* it was impossible to elude them.

Averroës put down his pen. He told himself (without too much conviction) that whatever we seek is never very far away. He put aside the manuscript of the *Tahāfut* and went over to the book shelf where the many volumes of the *Mohkam,* composed by blind Abensida and copied by Persian calligraphers, stood in a row. It was ludicrous to think that he might not have consulted them already, but he was tempted anew by the idle pleasure of turning their pages again: From this deliberate distraction he was in turn distracted by a kind of melody. He looked down over the railed balcony; below, in the narrow earthen patio, some half-clad boys were playing. One of them, standing on the shoulders of another, was obviously acting the part of the muezzin; with his eyes closed tight he chanted *There is no god but God*. The boy who sustained him, unmoving, was the minaret. A third, abjectly on his knees in the dust, was the congregation of the Faithful. The game did not last long: each one wanted to be the muezzin, no one cared to be the congregation or the tower. Averroës heard them arguing in *gross* dialect: that is, in the incipient Spanish of the Peninsula's Moslem plebs. He opened the *Quitah Ul Ain* of Jalal and thought proudly of how in all Córdoba (perhaps even in all Al-Andalus) there was not another copy of that perfect work, only this one which the emir Yacub Almansur had sent him from Tangier. The name of this seaport reminded him that the traveler Abulcasim Al-Ashari, who had just come back from Morocco, would be dining with him that evening at the home of the Koranic scholar Farach. Abulcasim claimed to have voyaged as far as the dominions of the Empire of Shin (China). His detractors, equipped with the peculiar logic supplied by hatred, swore that he had never set foot in China and that he had blasphemed against Allah in that country's temples. The gathering would, inevitably, last several hours. Hurriedly, Averroës resumed writing his *Tahāfut*. He worked until nightfall.

At Farach's house, the conversation went from a discussion of the incomparable virtues of the Governor to those of his brother the emir; later, in the garden, they spoke of roses. Abulcasim, who had not looked at them, swore that there were no roses like those which decorate the country houses of Andalusia. Farach did not let himself be flattered; he observed that the learned ibn-Qutaiba describes an excellent variety of perpetual rose which grows in the gardens of Hindustan and whose petals—blood red—have characters written on them saying: *There is no other god*

like God. Mohammed is the Apostle of God. He added that
Abulcasim surely knew of these roses. Abulcasim looked at
him with alarm. If he answered that he did, everyone would
judge him, justifiably, the readiest and most gratuitous of
imposters; if he replied that he did not, they would consider him an infidel. He chose to mumble that the keys to
occult matters are kept by the Lord, and that in all the
earth there is nothing, either green or faded, that is not
noted in His Book. These words are part of one of the first
sutras of the Koran, and they were received with a murmur
of reverence. Stimulated by this dialectical victory, Abulcasim was about to announce that the Lord is perfect in His
works, and inscrutable. Whereupon Averroës, prefiguring
the remote arguments of an as yet problematical Hume,
declared:

"It is easier for me to admit of an error in the learned
ibn-Qutaiba, or in the copyists, than admit that the earth
yields roses embodying a profession of Faith."

"Just so. Great words and true," said Abulcasim.

"One traveler speaks of a tree whose fruit are green
birds," recalled the poet Abdalmalik. "It would take a less
painful effort for me to believe in that tree than in roses
which bore words."

"The color of the birds," said Averroës, "would seem to
favor the first mentioned prodigy. Besides, fruits and birds
belong to the natural world, but writing is an art. To go
from leaves to birds is easier than to go from roses to
letters."

Another guest indignantly denied that writing was an art,
inasmuch as the original of the Koran—*the mother of the
Book*—is older than the Creation and is kept in Heaven.
Another man cited Chahiz of Basra, who had said that the
Koran is an essence which can take the form of a man or
of an animal, an opinion apparently in concord with the
theory that it has two faces. Farach then lengthily ex-

pounded the orthodox doctrine. The Koran, he said, is one of the attributes of God, like His mercy; it is copied in a book, it is pronounced with the tongue, it is remembered in one's heart, and the language and the signs and the writing are all works of man, while the Koran is eternal and irrevocable. Averroës, who had written a commentary on the *Republic,* could have mentioned that the mother of the Book is something on the order of its Platonic model, but he had already noticed that theology was a subject altogether inaccessible to Abulcasim.

Others, who had also noticed the same thing, urged Abulcasim to tell them the tale of some marvel. Then as now the world was an atrocious place; the audacious could move about in it, and so could the poor in spirit, the wretches who adjusted to anything. Abulcasim's memory was a mirror of intimate acts of cowardice. What tale could he tell? Besides, they demanded marvels of him, and marvels are probably not communicable; the moon in Bengal is not the same as the moon in the Yemen, though it be described by the same words. Abulcasim hesitated; then he spoke:

"Whoever travels through climes and cities," he unctuously announced, "will see many things worthy of credit. For instance, the following, which I have related only once before, to the King of the Turks. It took place at Sin Kalan (Canton), where the river of the Water of Life spills into the sea."

Farach asked if the city was to be found many leagues away from the Wall which had been built by Iskandar Zul Qarnain (Alexander Bicornis of Macedonia) to halt Gog and Magog.

"Deserts separate them," said Abulcasim, with involuntary arrogance. "It would take a *kafila* (a caravan) forty days to get within sight of its towers, and another forty days, they say, to reach it. I don't know of a single man in Sin Kalan who has ever seen the Wall, or who has ever seen anyone who did."

Terror of the crassly infinite, of mere space, of mere matter, laid a hand on Averroës for an instant. He gazed on the symmetrical garden; he knew himself grown old, useless, unreal. Abulcasim was saying:

"One afternoon, the Moslem merchants in Sin Kalan led me to a painted wood house inhabited by a large number of people. It is impossible to describe that house, which was more like a single room, with rows of chambers or of balconies, one on top of the other. People were eating and drinking in these cavities; the same activity was taking place on the floor and on a terrace. The people on the terrace played on drums and lutes, except for some score or so (who wore crimson masks) who were praying, singing, and conversing. They suffered imprisonment, but no one could see the prison: they rode on horseback, but no one saw the horse; they fought in combat, but their swords were reeds; they died and then stood up again."

"The activity of madmen," said Farach, "goes beyond the previsions of the sane."

"They were not mad," Abulcasim was forced to explain. "They were representing a story, a merchant told me."

No one understood, no one seemed to want to understand. In confusion, Abulcasim turned from the narrative which they had heard to cumbersome explanations. With the help of his hands, he said:

"Let us imagine that someone shows a story instead of telling it. Suppose this story is the one about the Seven Sleepers of Ephesus. We see them retire to the cave, we see them pray and sleep, sleep with their eyes open, we see them growing while they sleep, we see them awake at the end of three hundred and nine years, we see them awake in Paradise, we see them awake with the dog. Something of the sort was shown us that afternoon by the persons on the terrace."

"Did these people speak?" asked Farach.

"Of course they spoke," said Abulcasim, now become the apologist for a performance he scarcely remembered and which had only vexed him at the time. "They spoke and sang and perorated!"

"In that case," said Farach, "there was no need for *twenty* people. A single speaker can relate anything, however complex it may be."

Everyone approved this dictum. The virtues of Arabic were next extolled, for it is the language used by God to direct the angels; and Arabic poetry was praised. Abdalmalik, after properly considering the subject, held that the poets of Damascus or Córdoba who insisted on pastoral images and a Bedouin vocabulary were old-fashioned. He said it was absurd that a man before whose eyes the Guadalquivir ran wide should celebrate the still waters of a well. He urged the convenience of renovating the ancient metaphors; he stated that at the time Zuhair compared Destiny with a blind camel, this figure of speech could move people to astonishment, but that five centuries of wonder had exhausted the surprise. This dictum, too, was approved by all: they had heard it often, from many men. Averroës was silent. But at last he spoke, less for the sake of the others than for himself.

"With less eloquence," said Averroës, "but with arguments of the same order, I have defended the proposition now sustained by Abdalmalik. In Alexandria, they say that the only man incapable of a crime is the man who has already committed it and already repented; to be free of error, let us add, it is well to have professed it. In his *mohalaca*, Zuhair stated that in the course of eighty years of pain and glory he has often seen Destiny suddenly trample men, like a blind camel. Abdalmalik finds that this

figure of speech can no longer cause wonder. Many re-
joinders could be made to this objection. The first, that if
the end purpose of the poem was surprise, its life would be
measured not by centuries but by days and hours and even
perhaps by minutes. The second, that a renowned poet is less
an inventor than he is a discoverer. In praise of ibn-Sharaf
of Berja it has been said and repeated that only he could
imagine that the stars at dawn fall slowly, like leaves falling from a tree; if such an attribution were true, it would
be evidence that the image is worthless. An image one man
alone can compose is an image that touches no man. There
are an infinite number of things on earth; any one of them
can be equated to any other. To equate stars to leaves is no
less arbitrary than to equate them with fishes or birds. On
the other hand, there is no one who has not felt at some time
that Destiny is hard and awkward, that it is innocent and
also inhuman. It was with this conviction in mind, a conviction which may be ephemeral or may be continuous but
which no one may elude, that Zuhair's verse was written.
What was said in that verse will not ever be said better.
Besides (and perhaps here lies the essence of my reflections), time, which despoils fortresses, enriches verses. When
Zuhair composed his verse in Araby, it served to bring
two images face to face: the image of the old camel and
the image of Destiny. Repeated now, it serves to evoke the
memory of Zuhair and to fuse our regrets with those of the
dead Arabian. The figure had two terms then, and now it
has four. Time dilates the compass of verse, and I know of
some which, like music, are all things to all men. Thus,
when years ago in Marrakesh I was tormented by memories
of Córdoba, I took pleasure in repeating the apostrophe
Abdurrahman addressed to an African palm in the gardens
of Ruzafa:

> *You, too, O palm!*
> *are a stranger to this shore . . .*

And this is the singular merit of poetry: that words written by a King who longed for the East served me, an exile in Africa, in my nostalgia for Spain."

Averroës then spoke of the first poets, of those who in the Time of Ignorance, before Islam, already said everything there was to say and said it in the infinite language of the desert. Alarmed—not without reason—by ibn-Sharaf's ostentation, he pointed out that all poetry was summarized in the ancients and in the Koran, and he condemned the ambition to innovate as both illiterate and vainglorious. The other guests heard him with pleasure, for he vindicated tradition.

The muezzins were calling the Faithful to early morning prayer when Averroës entered his library again. (In the harem, the raven-haired slave girls had been torturing a red-haired slave girl, but Averroës wouldn't know about this until that afternoon.) The sense of the two equivocal words had somehow been revealed to him. With a firm and careful calligraphy he added the following lines to the manuscript.

Aristu (Aristotle) *calls panegyrics by the name of tragedy, and satires and anathemas he calls comedies. The Koran abounds in remarkable tragedies and comedies, and so do the* mohalacas *of the sanctuary.*

He felt sleepy, he felt a bit cold. He unwound his turban and looked at himself in a metal mirror. I do not know what his eyes saw, for no historian has ever described the forms of his face. I do know that he suddenly disappeared, as if fulminated by a bolt of flameless fire, and that with him disappeared the house and the invisible fountain and the books and the manuscripts and the doves and the many raven-haired slave girls and the quivering red-haired slave girl and Farach and Abulcasim and the rose trees and perhaps even the Guadalquivir.

In the foregoing story I have striven to narrate the process involved in a defeat. I thought, first, of the Bishop of Canterbury who proposed to demonstrate the existence of God; then, of the alchemists who sought the philosopher's stone; next, of the vain trisectors of the angle and squarers of the circle. Later I reflected that even more poetic is the case of the man who sets himself a goal not inaccessible to other men, but inaccessible to him. I remembered Averroës, who, circumscribed by the compass of Islam, could never know the significance of the words *tragedy* and *comedy*. I told the tale; as I progressed, I felt what the god mentioned by Buffon must have felt, the god who set out to create a bull and instead created a buffalo. I sensed that the work was making mock of me. I sensed that Averroës, striving to imagine a drama without ever having suspected what a theater was, was no more absurd than I, who strove to imagine Averroës with no material other than some fragments from Renan, Lane, and Asín Palacios. I sensed, on the last page, that my narrative was a symbol of the man I was while I wrote it, and that to write that story I had to be that man, and that to be that man I had to write that story, and so to infinity. (The instant I stop believing in him, "Averroës" disappears.)

—Translated by ANTHONY KERRIGAN

A SOLDIER OF URBINA

Beginning to fear his own unworthiness
for campaigns like the last he fought, at sea,
this soldier, resigning himself to minor duty,
wandered unknown in Spain, his own harsh country.

To get rid of or to mitigate the cruel
weight of reality, he hid his head in dream.
The magic past of Roland and the cycles
of Ancient Britain warmed him, made him welcome.

Sprawled in the sun, he would gaze on the widening
plain, its coppery glow going on and on;
he felt himself at the end, poor and alone,

not knowing what all the music had been hiding;
Suddenly, plunging deep in a dream of his own,
he came on Sancho and Don Quixote, riding.

—Translated by ALASTAIR REID

THE MAKER

He had never lingered over the pleasures of remembering. Impressions washed quickly over him, fleeting and vivid; the vermilion glaze of a potter, the firmament crowded with stars which were also gods, the moon, from which a lion had fallen, the smoothness of marble under gentle, feeling finger tips, the savor of boar's meat, which he loved to tear at with fierce, white teeth, a word of the Phoenician language, the black shadow thrown by a lance on the yellow sand, closeness of the sea or of women, the heavy wine whose harshness balanced the taste of honey, could, one and all, define the whole range of his spirit. Terror he knew, but at the same time rage and courage, and once he was the first to scale a wall held by the enemy. Eager, curious, offhand, without any other principle than satisfaction and its subsequent indifference, he traveled over the varying countries of the earth, and saw, on this or that coast line, the cities and palaces of men. In the teeming markets or at the foot of a mountain with a hazy summit, where centaurs might easily have lived, he had listened to involved tales, accepting them as he accepted reality itself, not questioning whether they were truths or fabrications.

Gradually, the universe in all its beauty was abandoning him; an obstinate mistiness obscured the lines in his hand, the sky was losing its population of stars, the earth under his feet was uncertain. Everything withdrew and became confused. When he realized that he was going blind, he wept; stoic resignation had not yet been invented, and Hector might flee without disgrace. "Now," he felt, "I shall not see the sky full of mythological visions, nor that face which the years will be transforming." Days and nights passed over his despairing flesh, but one morning he awoke, saw (free of shadows) the obscure things surrounding him, and felt inexplicably, as one might recognize music or a voice, that all this had happened to him before, and that he had faced it fearfully, but at the same time with joy, hope, and curiosity. Then he went deep into his memory, which seemed bottomless, and managed from that dizzying descent to retrieve the lost remembrance which shone like a coin in moonlight, perhaps because he had never faced it except possibly in a dream.

The memory was as follows: another youth had insulted him, and he had gone to his father and told him the story. His father let him talk, appearing neither to listen nor to understand; and then he took down from the wall a bronze dagger, handsome and charged with power, which the boy had secretly coveted. Now he held it in his hands, and the astonishment of possessing it wiped out the hurt he had suffered, but the voice of his father was saying "Let someone know you are a man," and there was a firmness in his voice. Night obscured the paths. Clasping the dagger, which he felt to be endowed with magic power, he descended the sharp slope surrounding the house and ran to the sea's edge, imagining himself Ajax and Perseus, and peopling the sea-smelling dark with wounds and battles. The precise flavor of that moment was what he was looking for now; the rest did not matter to him—the insults of the quarrel, the cumbersome fight, the return with the blood-stained blade.

Another memory, also involving night and an expectation of adventure, sprang up from that one. A woman, the first which the gods had offered him, had waited for him in the shade of a hypogeum, and he searched for her through corridors like webs of stone, and on slopes steeped in shadows. Why did these memories keep coming back to him, coming back like a simple prefiguration of the present?

With the final darkness, he understood. In that night of

his mortal eyes, into which he was now descending, both love and peril awaited him, Ares and Aphrodite, because now he was anticipating (because he was approaching closer) a hint of glory and of hexameters, a sense of men defending a temple which the gods would not save and of black ships searching at sea for a well-loved island, an inkling of the Odysseys and Iliads which he was destined to create and leave behind, resounding in the concavity of the human memory. We know these things; but not the things he felt as he descended into the ultimate darkness.

—Translated by ALASTAIR REID

EVERYTHING AND NOTHING

There was no one in him: behind his face (even the poor paintings of the epoch show it to be unlike any other) and behind his words (which were copious, fantastic, and agitated) there was nothing but a bit of cold, a dream not dreamed by anyone. At first he thought that everyone was like himself. But the dismay shown by a comrade to whom he mentioned this vacuity revealed his error to him and made him realize forever that an individual should not differ from the species. At one time it occurred to him that he might find a remedy for his difficulty in books, and so he learned the "small Latin, and less Greek," of which a contemporary spoke. Later, he considered he might find what he sought in carrying out one of the elemental rites of humanity, and so he let himself be initiated by Anne Hathaway in the long siesta hour of an afternoon in June. In his twenties, he went to London. Instinctively, he had already trained himself in the habit of pretending he was someone, so it should not be discovered that he was no one. In London, he found the profession to which he had been predestined, that of actor: someone who, on a stage, plays at being someone else, before a concourse of people who pretend to take him for that other one. His histrionic work taught him a singular satisfaction, perhaps the first he had ever known. And yet, once the last line of verse had been acclaimed and the last dead man dragged off stage, he tasted the hateful taste of unreality. He would leave off being Ferrex or Tamburlaine and become no one again. Thus beset, he took to imagining other heroes and other

115

tragic tales. And so, while his body complied with its bodily destiny in London bawdyhouses and taverns, the soul inhabiting that body was Caesar unheeding the augur's warnings, and Juliet detesting the lark, and Macbeth talking on the heath with the witches who are also the Fates. No one was ever so many men as that man: like the Egyptian Proteus he was able to exhaust all the appearances of being. From time to time, he left, in some obscure corner of his work, a confession he was sure would never be deciphered: Richard states that in his one person he plays many parts, and Iago curiously says "I am not what I am." The fundamental oneness of existing, dreaming, and acting inspired in him several famous passages.

He persisted in this directed hallucination for twenty years. But one morning he was overcome by a surfeit and horror of being all those kings who die by the sword and all those unfortunate lovers who converge, diverge, and melodiously expire. That same day he settled on the sale of his theater. Before a week was out he had gone back to his native village, where he recuperated the trees and the river of his boyhood, without relating them at all to the trees and rivers—illustrious with mythological allusion and Latin phrase—which his Muse had celebrated. He had to be someone: he became a retired impresario who has made his fortune and who is interested in making loans, in lawsuits, and in petty usury. It was in character, then, in this character, that he dictated the arid last will and testament we know, from which he deliberately excluded any note of pathos or trace of literature. Friends from London used to visit him in his retreat, and for them he would once more play the part of poet.

History adds that before or after his death he found himself facing God and said: *I, who have been so many men in vain, want to be one man, myself alone.* From out

of a whirlwind the voice of God replied: *I am not, either.
I dreamed the world the way you dreamed your work, my
Shakespeare: one of the forms of my dream was you, who,
like me, are many and no one.*

—*Translated by* ANTHONY KERRIGAN

FROM SOMEONE
TO NO ONE

In the beginning, God was the Gods (Elohim), a plural which some call the plural of majesty and others the plural of plenitude; some have thought they noted an echo of earlier polytheisms or a premonition of the doctrine, declared at Nicaea, that God is One and is Three. Elohim takes a single verb: the first verse of the Old Testament says literally: *In the beginning the Gods created* (singular) *the heaven and the earth.* Despite the vagueness suggested by the plural, Elohim is concrete and is called the God Jehovah, and we read that He walked in the garden in the cool of the day. Human traits define Him; and in one place in Scripture we read *It repented the Lord that he had made man on the earth, and it grieved him at his heart,* and in another place *for I the Lord thy God am a jealous God,* and in another *In the fire of my wrath have I spoken.* The subject of such locutions is indisputably Someone, a corporal Someone whom the centuries will magnify out of all focus. His titles are various: the Mighty One of Jacob, the Rock of Israel, I Am That I Am, God of Hosts, King of Kings. The last mentioned—which doubtless inspired, by antithesis, Gregory the Great's Serf of the Serfs of God— is, in the original, a superlative of king. "It is a property of the Hebrew tongue," says Fray Luis de León, "to thus double some same words, when an intensifier is wanted, either for good or ill. So that to say *Song of Songs* is the same as to say, in Castilian, *Song among Songs,* or *Man among Men,* that is, notable and eminent among all others and more excellent than many others." In the first centuries of our era, the theologians renovated the prefix *omni,* formerly reserved for adjectives concerned with nature or with Jupiter, and supplied the words *omnipotent, omnipresent, omniscient,* which make God into a respectable chaos of unimaginable superlatives. This nomenclature, like the others, seems to limit the divinity: toward the end of the fifth century, the unrevealed author of the *Corpus Dionysiacum* declares that no affirmative predicate is seemly for God. Nothing should be affirmed about Him, everything can be denied. Schopenhauer dryly notes: "This theology is the only true one, but it has no content." Composed in Greek, the treatises and letters which made up the *Corpus Dionysiacum* come to the attention of a ninth-century reader who turns them into Latin: he was Johannes Erigena or Scotus, that is, John Irish, whose name in history is Scotus Erigena, which is to say Irish Irish. Erigena formulates a doctrine of pantheistic cast: particular things are theophanies (revelations or apparitions of the divine) and behind them is God, the only reality, "but Who does not know what He is, because He is not a what, and is incomprehensible to Himself and to all intelligence." He is not wise, He is more than wise; He is not good, He is more than good; inscrutably He exceeds and rejects all attributes. John the Irishman, by way of defining God, has recourse to the word *nihilum,* which is nothingness; God is the primordial nothingness of the *creatio ex nihilo,* the abyss in which first the archetypes and then concrete beings were engendered. He is Nothing and No One. Those who conceived of Him in this way did so with the feeling that this condition is more than to be a Who or a What. Analogically, Shankara teaches that men, in deep sleep, are the universe of God.

The process I have just illustrated is not, certainly, fortuitous. Magnification to the point of nothingness comes about or tends to come about in all cults. We see it, unequivocally, in the case of Shakespeare. His contemporary, Ben Jonson, loves him "on this side Idolatry";

Dryden calls him the Homer of England's dramatic poets, but admits that he tends to be bombastic and vapid; the discursive eighteenth century strives to assay his virtues and censure his faults; in 1774, Maurice Morgan asserts that King Lear and Falstaff are no more than modifications of their creator's mind; at the beginning of the nineteenth century, this judgment is refurbished by Coleridge, for whom Shakespeare is no longer a man but a literary variant of the infinite God of Spinoza: ". . . his own nature as an individual person," he writes, ". . . was itself but a *natura naturata*—an effect, a product, not a power. It was Shakespeare's prerogative to have the universal, which is potentially in each particular, opened out to him, not as abstracted from the observation of a variety of men, but as the substance capable of endless modifications, of which his own personal existence was but one. . . ." Hazlitt corroborates or confirms that Shakespeare resembled all men. In himself he was nothing, but he was everything that all others are, or what they can be. Hugo, later, compared him with the ocean, which is a seedbed of possible forms.*

To be one thing is inexorably not to be all other things; the confused intuition of this truth has induced men to imagine that not to be is more than to be some thing, and that, in some way, it is to be everything. This fallacy is to be found in the words of that legendary king of Hindustan who renounces power and goes out to beg in the streets: "Henceforward I have no kingdom, or my kingdom is un-

---

* The same design is repeated in Buddhism. The first texts narrated that the Buddha, at the foot of the fig tree, intuits the infinite concatenation of all the causes and effects in the universe, the past and future incarnations of every being. The later texts, redacted centuries later, argue that nothing is real and that every understanding is fictitious and, further, that if there were as many Ganges rivers as there are grains of sand in the Ganges and as many Ganges again as there are grains of sand in the new Ganges rivers, the number of grains of sand would be less than the number of things the Buddha *does not know*.

limited; henceforward my body does not belong to me, or the entire earth belongs to me." Schopenhauer has written that history is an interminable and perplexed dream on the part of generations of humans; in the dream there are recurring forms; perhaps there are nothing but forms; one of them is the process described on this page.

—Translated by ANTHONY KERRIGAN

FORMS OF A LEGEND

People find the sight of an old man, an invalid, or a corpse, repugnant, and yet everyone is subject to death, illness, and old age. The Buddha declared that this thought led him to abandon his home and parents and put on the yellow robe of the ascetics, a testimony to be found in one of the books of the canon. Another book records the parable of the five secret messengers sent by the gods: a child, a stooped ancient, a cripple, a criminal on the rack, and a dead man, and they announce that our destiny is to be born, decline, fall ill, suffer just punishment, and die. The Judge of the Shadows (in the mythologies of Hindustan, Yama fulfills this function, inasmuch as he was the first man to die) asks the sinner whether he has not seen the messengers; the sinner admits that he has, but has not deciphered their admonishment; the myrmidons shut him up in a house full of fire. Perhaps the Buddha did not invent this menacing parable; it is enough for us to know that he stated it (*Majjhima nikaya,* 130) and that he may never, perhaps, have related it to his own life.

Reality may be too complex for oral transmission; legend recreates it in a manner which is only accidentally false and which allows it to go about the world, from mouth to mouth. In both the parable and the Buddha's declaration there figure an old man, an ill man, and a dead one; time made the two texts one, and made, out of the confusion, another story.

Siddhartha, the Bodhisattva, the pre-Buddha, is the son of a great king, Suddhodana, of the lineage of the sun. On the night of his conception his mother dreams that an elephant enters her right side, an elephant the color of

snow and with six tusks.* The interpretation put upon this
dream by the soothsayers is that the child would reign over
the world or would make the wheel of doctrine turn† and
show men how to free themselves from life and death. The
king would prefer that Siddhartha achieve temporal rather
than eternal greatness and he has the boy shut up in a
palace, from which all things that might reveal to him that
he is corruptible have been removed. In this situation
Siddhartha passes twenty-nine years of illusory happiness,
devoted to the pleasure of the senses. But one morning he
ventures out in his carriage and beholds with amazement a
man bent double, "whose hair is not like that of others,
whose body is not like that of others," who supports himself on a cane as he walks and whose flesh trembles. He
asks what manner of man is that. The coachman explains
that he is an old man and that all men on earth will become
as he is. Disquieted, Siddhartha gives orders for an immediate return to the palace. But then, in the course of a
new sally, he sees a man devoured by fever, covered with
the sores of leprosy and with ulcers. The coachman
explains that he is a sick man and that no one is exempt
from this danger. In still another sally, the prince sees a
man being borne on a bier. That inert figure, they explain,

---

* For us this dream is merely ugly. Not so for the Hindus: the elephant, a domestic animal, is a symbol of gentleness; the proliferation of
tusks could scarcely disquiet those used to viewing an art which, in order
to suggest that God is everything, fashions figures with multiple arms
and faces; six is a customary number (there are six ways of transmigra-
tion; six Buddhas anterior to Buddha; six cardinal points, counting the
zenith and the nadir; six divinities which the Yajur-Veda calls the six
portals of Brahma).

† This metaphor may have stimulated the Tibetans to invent the
prayer wheels: cylinders or wheels which gyrate around an axis, carrying
rolled up strips of paper with magic words upon them. Some of the
wheels are manually operated, others are like great mills, moved by water
or wind.

is a dead man, and to die is the law of all who are born. On yet another sally, the last, he sees a monk of the mendicant orders who does not desire either to live or to die; in his face there is peace; Siddhartha has found the way.

Hardy (*Der Buddhismus nach älteren Pali-Werken*) extolled the colorful quality of this legend; a contemporary Indologist, A. Foucher, whose mocking tone is not always intelligent or urbane, writes that, considering the prior ignorance of the Bodhisattva, the story is not lacking in dramatic climax and philosophic value. At the beginning of the fifth century of our era, the monk Fa-Hien went on a pilgrimage to the kingdoms of Hindustan in search of sacred books and he saw the ruins of the city of Kapilavastu and four statues which Asoka had erected to the north, south, east, and west of the walls in commemoration of the Bodhisattva's four encounters. At the beginning of the seventh century a Christian monk composed the novel called *Barlaam and Josaphat;* Josaphat (= Bodhisat, Bodhisattva) is the son of a king of India; the astrologers foretell that he will reign over a greater kingdom, the Kingdom of Glory; the king shuts him up in a palace, but Josaphat discovers the unfortunate condition of men specifically in the persons of a blind man, a leper, and a moribund man, and is converted, finally, to the faith by the hermit Barlaam. This Christian version of the legend was translated into many languages, including Dutch and Latin; at the instance of Hakon Hakonarson, a *Barlaams Saga* was created in Iceland in the middle of the thirteenth century. Cardinal Caesar Baronio included Josaphat in his revision (1585–90) of the Roman Martyrology. In 1615, Diego de Couto pointed out, in his continuation of the *Décadas,* the analogies between the feigned Indian fable and the true and pious history of Saint Josaphat. All this and much more may be found by the reader in the first volume of the *Origenes de la novela,* by Menéndez y Pelayo.

The legend which in Western lands determined that the Buddha be canonized by Rome possessed, nevertheless, one defect: the encounters which it postulates are effective, but also incredible. The four sallies of Siddhartha and the four didactic figures are not in concert with the habits of chance. Less attentive to esthetics than to the conversion of nations, the Doctors of the Church wished to justify the anomaly; Koeppen (*Die Religion des Buddha,* I, 82) notes that in the later form of the legend, the leper, the dead man, and the monk are simulacra which the divinities create for the instruction of Siddhartha. Thus, in the Third Book of the Sanskrit epic *Buddhacarita,* we read that the gods created a dead man, and that no one saw his body as it was borne along except the coachman and the Prince. In a legendary biography of the sixteenth century the four apparitions become four metamorphoses of a god (Wieger: *Vies chinoises du Buddha,* 37–41).

The *Lalitavistara* had gone even further. It is customary to speak with some scorn of this compilation of prose and verse written in an impure Sanskrit; in its pages the history of the Redeemer is distended until it becomes oppressive, until it produces vertigo. The Buddha, surrounded by twelve thousand monks and thirty-two thousand Bodhisattvas, reveals the text of the work to the gods; from out of the fourth heaven he fixed the era, the continent, the kingdom, and the caste into which he would be reborn to die for the last time; eighty thousand timbals accompany the words of his discourse, and the force of ten thousand elephants inform the body of his mother. The Buddha, in this strange poem, directs each stage of his destiny; he has the four divinities project the four symbolic figures and, when he interrogates the coachman, their identity and significance he already knows. Foucher sees this as an example of mere

servility on the part of the authors, who apparently
can not tolerate the Buddha's not knowing what a servant knows. To my mind, the enigma deserves another
solution. The Buddha creates the images and then asks
a third person their meaning. Theologically it would be
possible for this person to furnish the Buddha an answer,
for the book belongs to the school of Mahayana, which
teaches that the temporal Buddha is an emanation or
reflection of an eternal Buddha; the heavenly Buddha
directs all things, the temporal one suffers them or carries
them out. (Our century, possessed of another mythology
or vocabulary, speaks of the unconscious.) The human
nature of the Son, the Second Person of God, may cry out
from the Cross: *My God, my God, why hast Thou for-
saken me?*; the person of the Buddha, analogically, could
be dismayed by the forms his own divinity had created. . . .
But such dogmatic subtleties are not indispensable, however, for the unraveling of the problem. We need merely
remember that all religions in Hindustan, and Buddhism
most particularly, teach that the world is illusory. *Lalitavistara* means, according to Winternitz, *Detailed Account of
the Game* (of a Buddha); for Mahayana Buddhism,
the life of the Buddha on earth is a game or a dream,
and the earth itself another dream. Siddhartha chooses
his country and his parents. He fashions four forms which
will fill him with astonishment. He disposes that another
form declare the meaning of the first four. All this is
reasonable, if we assume that it is a dream of Siddhartha's;
even better if we think of it as a dream in which Siddhartha plays a part (as the leper and the monk play a
part), but a dream no one actually dreams, because,
in the eyes of Northern Buddhism,* the world and the

---

* Rhys Davids proscribes this locution, introduced by Burnouf, but its
use in this phrase is less cumbersome than that of the Great Passage or
Great Vehicle, which would have given the reader pause.

proselytes and Nirvana and the wheel of transmigrations and the Buddha are all equally unreal. No one is extinguished in Nirvana, as we read in a famous treatise, for the extinction of innumerable beings in Nirvana is like the disappearance of a phantasmagoria which a magician at a crossroads creates by occult art; in another place it is written that everything is mere emptiness, mere name, including the book which says so and the man who reads it. Paradoxically, the poem's numerical excesses—twelve thousand monks and thirty-two thousand Bodhisattvas—do not add, but rather take away reality. The vast forms and the vast ciphers (Chapter XII includes a series of twenty-three words which indicate the unit followed by an increasing number of zeros, from 9 to 49, 51 and 53) are only vast and monstrous bubbles, emphasizing Nothingness. Thus the unreal progressively riddles the story; first it made the figures fantastic, then it did the same to the prince, and, along with the prince, all ages and the universe itself.

At the end of the nineteenth century, Oscar Wilde proposed a variant: the happy prince dies in the seclusion of the palace without having discovered sorrow, but his posthumous effigy discerns it from the height of his pedestal.

The chronology of Hindustan is uncertain; my erudition is even more so; Koeppen and Hermann Beckh are perhaps as fallible as the compiler who risks the present note; I should not be surprised if my story of the legend were legendary, compounded of substantial truth and accidental errors.

—*Translated by* ANTHONY KERRIGAN

THE ZAHIR

In Buenos Aires, the Zahir is a common ordinary coin worth twenty centavos; the letters N T and the number 2 are notched by razor or penknife marks; 1929 is engraved on the obverse side. (In Guzerat, toward the end of the eighteenth century, a tiger was Zahir; in Java, it was a blind man in the Surakarta mosque, a man whom the Faithful stoned; in Persia, an astrolabe which Nadir Shah ordered sunk to the bottom of the sea; in the prisons of Madhi, about 1892, it was a small compass, wrapped in a strip of turban, which Rudolph Carl von Slatin handled; in the mosque at Córdoba, it was, according to Zotenberg, a vein running through the marble in one of the twelve hundred columns; in the Jewish quarter of Tetuán, it was the bottom of a well.) Today is the thirteenth of November; on the seventh of June, at dawn, the Zahir fell into my hands; I am not now the person I was on that day, but still I am able to remember, and perhaps even to relate, what happened. I am still, however partially, Borges.

Teodelina Villar died on the sixth of June. Around 1930, her various likenesses filled the smart reviews; this ubiquity probably contributed to the legend that she was beautiful, although not every one of her effigies unconditionally supported this hypothesis. In any case, Teodelina Villar was less interested in beauty than in perfection. The Hebrews and the Chinese codified the entire human condition; in the *Mishnah* it is written that, after sunset on Saturday, a tailor should not go out into the street with so much as a needle about him; in the *Book of Rites* it is stated that a guest should wear a grave air when accepting the first glass of wine, and adopt a happily respectful mien on taking the second. Teodelina Villar imposed on herself an analogous

128

but even more minutely rigorous program. Like an adept of Confucius or of the Talmud, she sought irreproachable correctness in every act; her striving was more admirable than theirs, however, and sterner, for the norms of her credo were not eternal, but rather depended on the chance code of Paris or Hollywood. Teodelina Villar let herself be seen in the orthodox places, at the orthodox time, with the orthodox attributes, and the orthodox boredom, but the boredom, the attributes, the time and the places all faded and became passé almost at once, and only served Teodelina Villar to define poor taste. She sought the Absolute, like Flaubert, but the Absolute in the momentary. Her life was exemplary, and yet an inner despair unremittingly gnawed her. She attempted continual metamorphoses, as if to flee from herself; the color of her hair and the forms of her hair-do were notoriously unstable. She was always changing her smile, her complexion, the slant of her eyes. Beginning in 1932 she was studiously thin. . . . The war gave her pause. How to follow the fashion when Paris was occupied by the Germans? A foreigner whom she had always distrusted took advantage of her good faith to sell her a lot of cylindrical hats; within the year she found out that these absurd creations *had never been worn in Paris* and therefore were not hats at all but arbitrary and unauthorized aberrations. Disasters never occur singly: Doctor Villar was forced to move to Calle Aráoz, and his daughter's likeness came to decorate advertisements for creams and automobiles. (The creams which she applied to excess, the automobiles she *no longer* owned!) She knew that the exercise of her art required a fortune. She chose to retire rather than to bungle. Besides, it pained her to have to compete with giddy girls. The sinister apartment on Aráoz proved too much for her to bear: on June 6, Teodelina Villar committed the solecism of dying in the southern suburbs. Shall I confess that, moved by the sincerest of

Argentine passions—snobbism—I was enamored of her, and that her death moved me to tears? Perhaps the reader has already suspected as much.

At a wake, the progress of corruption causes the dead to recuperate their former faces. At some stage or other of the confused night of the sixth, Teodelina Villar magically became what she had been twenty years before; her features recovered the authority supplied by hauteur, money, youth, the awareness of crowning a hierarchy, a lack of imagination, a certain limitation, stolidity. I thought, more or less, thus: no version of this face, which had so unsettled me, will be as memorable as the one I now saw; better that it be the last, especially since it could have been the first. I left her lying rigidly among the flowers, her disdain of death achieving perfection. It was perhaps two in the morning when I went away. Outside, the predictable rows of one- and two-story houses had taken on the abstract air they assume at night, when shadow and silence simplify them. Inebriated with an almost impersonal pity, I roamed the streets. At the corner of Chile and Tacuarí I saw that a wine shop was open. And in that wine shop—to my detriment—three men were playing cards.

The figure of speech known as *oxymoron* consists in applying to a word an epithet which seems to contradict the word itself: thus the Gnostics spoke of dark light, the alchemists of a black sun. To make my last visit to Teodelina Villar and then to go out and order a drink in a wine shop was a kind of oxymoron; I was tempted by the coarseness and ease with which I could do it. (The fact that a card game was in progress served to heighten the contrast.) I ordered a glass of orange brandy. In my change I was given the Zahir. I stared at it for a moment, and then I went out into the street, perhaps already feverish. It occurred to me that every coin in the world is a symbol for all the coins that forever glitter in history and in fable. I recalled the obol of Charon; and the obol which Belisarius sought; Judas' thirty pieces; the drachmas of Laïs, the courtesan; the ancient coin proffered by one of the Seven Sleepers of Ephesus; the shining coins of the wizard of *The Thousand and One Nights,* which turned into paper circles; Isaac Laquedem's inexhaustible penny; the 60,000 pieces of silver—one for each line of an epic poem—which Firdusi returned to a king because they were not gold; the gold piece which Ahab had nailed to the mast; Leopold Bloom's irreversible florin; the louis d'or whose effigy informed against the fugitive Louis XVI close by Varennes. As in a dream the thought that every coin allows such illustrious connotations struck me as of a vast, if inexplicable, importance. I walked with increasing haste down deserted streets and through empty squares. Fatigue deposited me at some corner or other. I recognized a long-suffering iron fence. Behind it I saw the black and white tiles of the portico of the Church of La Concepción. I had wandered about in a random circle. I now found myself a block from the wine shop where I had been given the Zahir.

I turned the corner. The dark octagonal window indicated from a distance that the shop was closed. In Calle Belgrano, I took a cab. Sleepless, obsessed, almost joyful, I reflected on how nothing is less material than money, inasmuch as any coin whatsoever (a twenty-centavo piece, let us say) is, strictly speaking, a repertory of possible futures. Money is abstract, I repeated, money is future time. It can be an evening in the suburbs, it can be the music of Brahms, it can be maps, it can be chess, it can be coffee, it can be the words of Epictetus teaching us to despise gold. Money is a Proteus more versatile than the one on the island of Pharos. It is unpredictable time, Bergsonian time, not the obstinate time of Islam or of the Portico. The determinists deny that there is such a thing as a single possible act in the world, that is, an act which might have happened.

But a coin symbolizes our free will. (I did not yet suspect that these "thoughts" of mine were a stratagem I was opposing to the Zahir and the first form of its demoniacal influence.) I fell asleep after tenacious caviling, but dreamt I was a heap of gold coin guarded by a griffin.

The next day I decided I had been drunk. I also decided to be rid of the coin which so unnerved me. I looked at it: there was nothing out of the ordinary about it, except for the notched cuts. The best thing to do would have been to bury it in the garden or hide it in some corner of the library, but I was anxious to get out of its orbit. I preferred to lose it. I did not go, that morning, to the Church of El Pilar, nor to the cemetery; instead I went by subway to Constitución, and from Constitución to the corner of San Juan and Boedo. I got off, on an impulse, at Urquiza. I set out in a southwesterly direction. With studied lack of order I turned one corner and then another and another, and, in a street that looked to me like any other, I went into some dive or other, ordered a drink, and paid for it with the Zahir. I half closed my eyes, behind my dark glasses, and managed not to see the numbers on the houses nor the name of the street. That night I took a sleeping pill and slept easily.

The composition of a tale of fantasy served to distract me until the end of June. This tale involves two or three enigmatic periphrases: in place of *blood* I wrote *sword's water; gold* is *serpent's bed*. And the story is told in the first person. The narrator is an ascetic who has renounced all dealings with men and who lives in a kind of desert. (The name of this place is Gnitaheidr.) He leads a simple, candid life, and some people, therefore, consider him an angel; such a view is a pious exaggeration, for no man is free of sin. To go no further afield, our man has cut his father's throat; true enough, the father was a famous wizard and had gotten his hands on an infinite treasure by the use of magical arts. Our man, then, has now dedicated his life to guarding this treasure from the insane greed of humankind. He stands watch day and night. Soon, perhaps too soon, his vigil will come to an end: the stars have revealed to him that the sword which will cut it short has already been forged. (The name of the sword is Gram.) In an increasingly tortuous style, he considers the sheen and suppleness of his own body; in some paragraph or other he speaks distractedly of body scales; in still another he states that the treasure he guards is a hoard of fulgent gold and reddish rings. Finally we realize that the ascetic is the serpent Fafnir and that the treasure on which he lies is the Treasure of the Nibelungs. The appearance of Sigurd brings the story to an abrupt end.

As I have already said, the composition of this trifle (in the course of whose narrative I intercalated, with pseudo-erudition, an occasional line from the *Fáfnismál*) allowed me to forget the existence of the coin. Some nights I felt so sure of being able to forget it, that I voluntarily summoned it to mind. The truth is that I overdid these intervals: it proved easier to start the process than to put an end to it. In vain did I repeat that this abominable nickel disc differed in no wise from all those others that are passed from hand to hand, all alike, infinite and inoffensive. Impelled by this reflection, I strove to think of another coin, but was unable. I remember, too, some frustrating experiments with Chilean five- and ten-centavo coins and with an Uruguayan *vintén*. On the sixteenth of July, I acquired a pound sterling; I did not look at it all day long, but that night (and many others) I placed it under a magnifying glass and studied it by the light of a powerful electric lamp. Then, with a pencil, I traced it on paper. Neither the bright gold of the coin nor the dragon of St. George was any use: I could not get rid of my obsession.

Sometime in August I made up my mind to consult a

psychiatrist. I did not tell him the whole ridiculous story; I simply said that I was tormented by insomnia and that I was often haunted by the image of some object or other; the image, for example, of a poker chip or of a coin. . . . Shortly afterward, in a book shop in Calle Sarmiento, I dug up a copy of Julius Barlach's *Urkunden zur Geschichte der Zahirsage* (Breslau, 1899).

My ill was described in that book. According to the prologue the author proposed "to gather into one handy octavo volume all the documents relating to the superstition of the Zahir, including four items from the Habicht archives and the original manuscript of the Philip Meadows Taylor report." The belief in the Zahir is Islamic and apparently dates from the eighteenth century. (Barlach calls into question the passages which Zotenburg attributes to Abul-feda.) In Arabic, *Zahir* means notorious, visible; in this sense, it is one of the ninety-nine names of God; in Moslem lands, the people use it to designate "beings or things which possess the terrible virtue of being unforgettable, and whose image finally drives people mad." Our first irrefutable testimony on this head comes from the Persian Lutf Alí Azur. This polygraph and dervish wrote, in the punctilious pages of the biographical encyclopedia titled *Temple of Fire*, that in a school at Shiraz there was a copper astrolabe "fashioned in such wise that whoever looked at it even once could afterwards think of nothing else, whereupon the King ordered it thrown into the deepest part of the sea, lest men forget the universe." The account furnished by Meadows Taylor—who was in the service of the Nizam of Hyderabad and wrote the well-known *Confessions of a Thug*—is more extensive. Around 1832, in the outskirts of Bhuj, Taylor heard the unusual phrase "Verily he has looked on the Tiger," by way of signifying madness or sanctity. He was told that the reference was to a magic tiger, a tiger which had signified the ruin of whoever had looked on it, even if it had been from afar, for the beholder was left sunken in thought until the end of his days. Someone said that one of these unfortunates had fled to Mysore, where he had painted the figure of the tiger in a palace. Years later, Taylor visited the prisons of this kingdom; at Nittur, the governor showed him a cell on whose floor, walls, and vaulting a Moslem fakir had designed—in barbaric colors which time was mellowing before their complete erasure—a species of infinite Tiger. This Tiger was made up of many tigers fused in the most vertiginous manner: this Tiger was traversed by tigers, striped with tigers, and encompassed seas and armies and Himalayas resembling tigers. The painter had died years before in this same cell; he had come from Sind or perhaps Guzerat and his initial idea had been to trace out a map of the world. Some vestiges of this intent were to be seen in the monstrous image. Taylor recounted the story to Mohammad Al-Yemeni, of Fort William. This man told him that every created being tends toward *Zaheer,** but that the All-Merciful does not allow two things to be Zaheer at the same time inasmuch as one alone is enough to fascinate a multitude; he added that there is always a Zaheer, that in the Age of Ignorance it was the idol called Yauq, and that later it was a prophet from Jorasan who used to wear a veil embroidered with stones or a mask of gold;† he also said that God is inscrutable.

I read Barlach's monograph several times. I need not publicly plumb the depth of my feelings; I recall my despair when I realized that nothing could save me now, my essential relief in knowing that I was not to blame for my misfortune, the envy I felt toward those whose Zahir was

---

* Taylor's spelling.

† Barlach observes that Yauq is mentioned in the Koran (71, 23); that the prophet is Al-Mokanna (the Veiled One); and that no one except Philip Meadows Taylor's astonishing informant ever linked them to the Zahir.

not a coin but a fragment of marble or a tiger. How easy to avoid thinking about a tiger! I also recall the singular anxiety with which I read the following paragraph: "A commentator on the *Gulshan i Raz* declares that whoever has laid eyes on the Zahir will soon see the Rose, and he cites a line of verse interpolated into Attar's *Asrar Nama* (Book of Things Unknown): 'The Zahir is the shadow of the Rose and the rending of the Veil.' "

I had been surprised, on the night they waked Teodelina, not to see among those present the Señora de Abascal, her younger sister. In October, a friend of hers told me:

"Poor Julia! She grew very strange, and they had to put her away in the Bosch Sanitarium. Imagine! The nurses have to spoon feed her. She goes on about coins, that's her obsession. Just like Morena Sackmann's chauffeur."

Time, which attenuates memories, only aggravates that of the Zahir. There was a time when I could visualize first the obverse and then the reverse. Now I see them both simultaneously. It's not as if the Zahir were made of glass, for one face is not superimposed upon the other; it's rather as if one's vision was spherical and as if the Zahir floated in the middle. Whatever is not the Zahir appears before me in a faded, far-off form: for instance, the disdainful image of Teodelina, or physical pain. Tennyson said that if we could understand a single flower we would know who we are and what the world is. Perhaps he meant that there is no deed, however so humble, which does not implicate universal history and the infinite concatenation of causes and effects. Perhaps he meant that the visible world is implicit, in its entirety, in each manifestation, just as, in the same way, will, according to Schopenhauer, is implicit, in its entirety, in each individual. The cabalists considered man a microcosm, a symbolic mirror of the universe; according to Tennyson, everything would be that; even the intolerable Zahir.

Julia's fate will have overtaken me before 1948. I will have to be fed and dressed; I will not know whether it is morning or evening; I will not know who Borges was. To call this prospect terrible would be fallacious, since none of the circumstances will touch me. One might as well speak of the terrible pain endured by an anesthetized man when his skull is opened. I shall no longer perceive the universe; I shall perceive only the Zahir. The Idealists maintain that the verbs "to live" and "to dream" are strictly synonymous. I shall pass from thousands of apparitions to one alone: from a very complex dream to a very simple dream. Others will dream that I am mad, and I shall dream of the Zahir. And when everyone on earth thinks of the Zahir day and night, which will be a dream and which a reality, the earth or the Zahir?

I am still able to walk about the streets in the empty hours of the night. Dawn often surprises me sitting on a bench in the Plaza Garay, thinking (trying to think) of the passage in the *Asrar Nama* which says the Zahir is the shadow of the Rose and the rending of the Veil. I associate that judgment with the report that the Sufis, attempting to lose themselves in God, repeat their own name or the ninety-nine names of the divinity until they lose all meaning. I long to tread the same path. Perhaps I will manage to wear away the Zahir by force of thinking of it and thinking of it. Perhaps behind the Zahir I shall find God.

—Translated by Anthony Kerrigan

THE ALEPH

O God, I could be bounded in a nut-
shell and count myself a King of infinite space.
—*Hamlet*, II, 2.

But they will teach us that Eternity
is the Standing still of the Present
Time, a *Nunc-stans* (as the Schools
call it); which neither they, nor any
else understand, no more than they
would a *Hic-stans* for an Infinite
greatness of Place.
—*Leviathan*, IV, 46.

On the incandescent February morning Beatriz Viterbo
died, after a death agony so imperious it did not for a
moment descend into sentimentalism or fear, I noticed that
the iron billboards in the Plaza Constitución bore new
advertisements for some brand or other of Virginia tobacco;
I was saddened by this fact, for it made me realize that the
incessant and vast universe was already moving away from
her and that this change was the first in an infinite series.
The universe would change but I would not, I thought with
melancholy vanity; I knew that sometimes my vain devo-
tion had exasperated her; now that she was dead, I could
consecrate myself to her memory, without hope but also
without humiliation. I thought of how the thirtieth of
April was her birthday; to visit her house in Calle Garay
on that day and pay my respects to her father and Carlos
Argentino Daneri, her first cousin, would be an act of
courtesy, irreproachable and perhaps even unavoidable. I
would wait, once again, in the twilight of the overladen
entrance hall, I would study, one more time, the particulars

of her numerous portraits: Beatriz Viterbo in profile, in color; Beatriz wearing a mask, during the Carnival of 1921; Beatriz at her First Communion; Beatriz on the day of her wedding to Roberto Alessandri; Beatriz a little while after the divorce, at a dinner in the Club Hípico; Beatriz with Delia San Marco Porcel and Carlos Argentino; Beatriz with the Pekingese which had been a present from Villegas Haedo; Beatriz from the front and in a three-quarter view, smiling, her hand under her chin. . . . I would not be obliged, as on other occasions, to justify my presence with moderate-priced offerings of books, with books whose pages, finally, I learned to cut beforehand, so as to avoid finding, months later, that they were still uncut.

Beatriz Viterbo died in 1929. From that time on, I never let a thirtieth of April go by without a visit to her house. I used to arrive there around seven-fifteen and stay about twenty-five minutes. Every year I came a little later and stayed a little longer. In 1933 a torrential rain worked to my advantage: they were forced to invite me to dine. I did not fail to avail myself of this advantageous precedent. In 1934, I appeared, just after eight, with a honey nutcake from Santa Fe. With the greatest naturalness, I remained for supper. And thus, on these melancholy and vainly erotic anniversaries, Carlos Argentino Daneri began gradually to confide in me.

Beatriz was tall, fragile, lightly leaning forward: there was in her walk (if the oxymoron is acceptable) a kind of gracious torpor, the beginnings of an ecstasy. Carlos Argentino is rosy, important, gray-haired, fine-featured. He holds some subordinate position or other in an illegible library in the south side suburbs. He is authoritarian, but also ineffective. Until very recently, he took advantage of nights and holidays to avoid going out of his house. At a remove of two generations, the Italian *s* and the copious gesticulation of the Italians survive in him. His mental activity is continuous, impassioned, versatile, and altogether insignificant. He abounds in useless analogies and fruitless scruples. He possesses (as did Beatriz) long, lovely, tapering hands. For several months he was obsessed with Paul Fort, less with his ballads than with the idea of irreproachable glory. "He is the Prince of the poets of France," he would repeat fatuously. "You will set yourself against him in vain; no, not even your most poisoned barb will reach him."

The thirtieth of April, 1941, I allowed myself to add to the gift of honey nutcake a bottle of Argentine cognac. Carlos Argentino tasted it, judged it "interesting," and, after a few glasses, launched on a vindication of modern man.

"I evoke him," he said with rather inexplicable animation, "in his studio-laboratory, in the city's watchtowers, so to say, supplied with telephones, telegraphs, phonographs, radiotelephone apparatus, cinematographic equipment, magic lanterns, glossaries, timetables, compendiums, bulletins. . . ."

He remarked that for a man of such faculties the act of travel was useless. Our twentieth century had transformed the fable of Mohammed and the mountain: the mountains, now, converged upon the modern Mohammed.

His ideas seemed so inept to me, their exposition so pompous and so vast, that I immediately related them to literature: I asked him why he did not write them down. Foreseeably he replied that he had already done so: these concepts, and others no less novel, figured in the Augural Canto, or more simply, the Prologue Canto, of a poem on which he had been working for many years, without publicity, without any deafening to-do, putting his entire reliance on those two props known as work and solitude. First, he opened the floodgates of the imagination; then he made use of a sharp file. The poem was titled *The Earth*; it consisted of a description of the planet, wherein, naturally, there was no lack of picturesque digression and elegant apostrophe.

I begged him to read me a passage, even though brief. He opened a drawer in his desk, took out a tall bundle of pages from a pad, each sheet stamped with the letterhead of the Juan Crisóstomo Lafinur Library, and, with sonorous satisfaction, read out:

I have seen, like the Greek, the cities of men and their fame,
Their labor, days of various light, hunger's shame;
I correct no event, falsify no name,
But the voyage *I narrate is* . . . autour de ma chambre.

"By all lights an interesting strophe," he opined. "The first line wins the applause of the professor, the academician, the Hellenist, if not of superficial pedants, who form, these last, a considerable sector of public opinion. The second passes from Homer to Hesiod (the entire verse an implicit homage, writ on the façade of the resplendent building, to the father of didactic poetry), not without rejuvenating a procedure whose lineage goes back to Scripture, that of enumeration, congeries or conglomeration. The third line— Baroquism? Decadentism? Purified and fanatical cult of form?—is composed of two twin hemistichs. The fourth, frankly bilingual, assures me the unconditional support of every spirit sensitive to the gay lure of graceful play. I say nothing of the rare rhyme, nor of the learning which permits me—without any pedantry!—to accumulate, in four lines, three erudite allusions encompassing thirty centuries of compressed literature: first to the *Odyssey,* second to *Works and Days,* third to the immortal bagatelle proffered us through the idling of the Savoyard's pen. . . . Once more I have understood that modern art requires the balsam of laughter, the *scherzo.* Decidedly, Goldoni has the floor!"

He read me many another stanza, each of which obtained his approbation and profuse commentary, too. There was

nothing memorable in any of them. I did not even judge
them very much worse than the first one. There had been a
collaboration, in his writing, between application, resignation, and chance; the virtues which Daneri attributed to
them were posterior. I realized that the poet's labor lay
not with the poetry, but with the invention of reasons to
make the poetry admirable; naturally, this ulterior and subsequent labor modified the work for him, but not for others.
Daneri's oral style was extravagant; his metric heaviness
hindered his transmitting that extravagance, except in a
very few instances, to the poem.*

Only once in my life have I had occasion to examine the
fifteen thousand dodecasyllabic verses of the *Poly-Olbion*,
that topographic epic poem in which Michael Drayton recorded the flora, fauna, hydrography, orography, military
and monastic history of England; I am sure that this considerable, but limited, production is less tedious than the
vast congeneric enterprise of Carlos Argentino. The latter
proposed to put into verse the entire face of the planet;
in 1941, he had already dispatched several hectares of the
State of Queensland, in addition to one kilometer of the
course of the River Ob, a gasometer north of Veracruz, the
main business houses in the parish of La Concepción, the
villa owned by Mariana Cambaceres de Alvear on Eleventh
of September street, in Belgrano, and an establishment devoted to Turkish baths not far from the famous Brighton

---

* I recall, nevertheless, the following lines from a satire in which he
harshly fustigated bad poets:

> This one gives his poem bellicose armorings
> Of erudition; that one puts in pomp and jubilee.
> Both in vain beat their ridiculous wings . . .
> Forgetting, the wretches, the factor BEAUTY!

Only the fear of creating for himself an army of implacable and
powerful foes dissuaded him (he told me) from fearlessly publishing
this poem.

Aquarium. He read me from his poem certain laborious passages concerning the Australian zone; these large and formless alexandrines lacked the relative agitation of the Preface. I copy one stanza:

> *Know ye. To the right hand of the routinary post*
> (*Coming, of course, from the North-northwest*)
> *One wearies out a skeleton—Color? White-celeste—*
> *Which gives the sheep run an ossuary cast.*

"Two audacious strokes," he cried out in exultation, "redeemed, I can hear you muttering, by success! I admit it, I admit it. One, the epithet *routinary,* which accurately proclaims, *en passant,* the inevitable tedium inherent in pastoral and farming chores, a tedium which neither georgic poetry nor our already laureled *Don Segundo* ever ventured to denounce in this way, in red-hot heat. The other, the energetic prosaicism of *one wearies out a skeleton,* a phrase which the prudish will want to excommunicate in horror, but which the critic with virile taste will appreciate more than his life. For the rest, the entire line is of high carat, the highest. The second hemistich engages the reader in the most animated converse; it anticipates his lively curiosity, places a question in his mouth and answers it . . . instantly. And what do you tell me of that find of mine: *white-celeste?* This picturesque neologism insinuates the sky, which is a very important factor in the Australian landscape. Without this evocation, the colors of the sketch would be much too somber, and the reader would find himself compelled to close the book, wounded in the innermost part of his soul by a black and incurable melancholy."

Toward midnight, I took my leave.

Two Sundays later, Daneri called me on the telephone, for the first time in his life, I believe. He proposed that we meet at four o'clock, "to drink a glass of milk together, in the salon-bar next door, which the progressivism of

Zunino and of Zungri—the proprietors of my house, you will recall—is causing to be inaugurated on the corner. Truly, a confectionery shop you will be interested in knowing about." I accepted, with more resignation than enthusiasm. There was no difficulty in finding a table; the "salon-bar," inexorably modern, was just slightly less atrocious than what I had foreseen; at the neighboring tables an excited public mentioned the sums which Zunino and Zungri had invested without batting an eye. Carlos Argentino feigned astonishment over some wonder or other in the lighting installations (which he doubtless already knew about), and he said to me, with a certain severity:

"You'll have to admit, no matter how grudgingly, that these premises vie successfully with the most renowned of Flores."

Then, he reread me four or five pages of his poem. He had made corrections in accordance with a depraved principle of verbal ostentation: where he had formerly written *azurish,* he now put *azuritic, azuritish,* and even *azury.* The word *lacteous* proved not ugly enough for him; in the course of an impetuous description of a wool washer, he preferred *lactary, lactinous, lactescent, lactiferous.* . . . He bitterly reviled the critics; later, in a more benign spirit, he compared them to persons "who dispose of no precious metals, nor steam presses, nor rolling presses, nor sulphuric acids for minting treasures, but who can *indicate* to *others* the *site* of a treasure." Next he censured *prologomania* "which the Prince of Talents, in the graceful prefacing of his *Don Quixote,* already ridiculed." He nevertheless admitted to me now that by way of frontispiece to the new work a showy prologue, an accolade signed by the feather pen of a bird of prey, of a man of weight, would be most convenient. He added that he planned to bring out the initial cantos of his poems. I understood, then, the singular telephonic invitation; the man was going to ask me to preface his pedantic farrago. My fears proved unfounded: Carlos Argentino observed, with rancorous admiration, that he did not misuse the epithet in denominating as *solid* the prestige achieved in all circles by Álvaro Melián Lafinur, man of letters, who would, if I insisted on it, delightfully prologue the poem. So as to avoid the most unpardonable of failures, I was to make myself spokesman for two undeniable merits: formal perfection and scientific rigor, "inasmuch as this vast garden of tropes, figures of speech, and elegance, allows no single detail which does not confirm the severe truth." He added that Beatriz had always enjoyed herself with Álvaro.

I assented, assented profusely. For greater conviction, I promised to speak to Álvaro on Thursday, rather than wait until the following Monday: we could meet at the small supper that usually climaxes every reunion of the Writers' Club. (There are no such suppers, but it is an irrefutable fact that the reunions do take place on Thursdays, a point which Carlos Argentino Daneri would find confirmed in the daily newspapers, and which lent a certain reality to the phrase.) Adopting an air halfway between divinatory and sagacious, I told him that before taking up the question of a prologue, I would delineate the curious plan of the book. We took our leave of each other. As I turned the corner into Calle Bernardo de Irigoyen, I impartially considered the alternatives before me: a) I could talk to Álvaro and tell him how that cousin of Beatriz' (this explicatory euphemism would allow me to say her name) had elaborated a poem which seemed to dilate to infinity the possibilities of cacophony and chaos; b) I could fail to speak to Álvaro altogether. 1 foresaw, lucidly, that my indolence would choose b.

From early Friday morning the telephone began to disquiet me. It made me indignant to think that this instrument, which in other days had produced the irrecoverable voice of Beatriz, could lower itself to being a receptacle for the useless and perhaps even choleric complaints of that deceived man Carlos Argentino Daneri. Luckily, nothing awful occurred—except the inevitable animosity inspired by that man, who had imposed on me a delicate mission and would later forget me altogether.

The telephone lost its terrors; but then toward the end of October, Carlos Argentino called me again. He was terribly agitated; at first I could not identify the voice. Sadly and yet wrathfully he stammered that the now uncurbed Zunino and Zungri, under the pretext of enlarging their outrageous confectionery, were going to demolish his house.

"The house of my fathers! My house, the inveterate house of the Calle Garay!" he went on repeating, perhaps forgetting his grief in the melody.

It was not difficult for me to share his grief. Once past forty, every change is a detestable symbol of the passage of time. Besides, at stake was a house that, for me, infinitely alluded to Beatriz. I wanted to bring out this most delicate point; my interlocutor did not hear me. He said that if Zunino and Zungri persisted in their absurd proposal, Doctor Zunni, his lawyer, would enter an action *ipso facto* for damages and would oblige them to pay one hundred thousand *pesos nacionales* in compensation.

I was impressed to hear the name of Zunni: his practice, out of his office at the corner of Caseros and Tacuarí, was of a proverbial and solemn reliability. I asked if Zunni had already taken charge of the matter. Daneri said he would speak to him that very afternoon. He hesitated, and then, in that level, impersonal voice to which we all have recourse for confiding something very intimate, he told me that in order to finish the poem the house was indispensable to him, for in one of the cellar corners there was an Aleph. He indicated that an Aleph is one of the points in space containing all points.

"It's in the dining-room cellar," he explained, his diction

grown hasty from anxiety. "It's mine, it's mine; I discovered it in childhood, before I was of school age. The cellar stair is steep, and my aunt and uncle had forbidden me to go down it. But someone said that there was a world in the cellar. They were referring, I found out later, to a trunk, but I understood there was a world there. I descended secretly, went rolling down the forbidden stairs, fell off. When I opened my eyes I saw the Aleph."

"The Aleph?" I echoed.

"Yes, the place where, without any possible confusion, all the places in the world are found, seen from every angle. I revealed my discovery to no one, and I returned there. The child could not understand that this privilege was proffered him so that the man might chisel out the poem! Zunino and Zungri will not dislodge me, no, a thousand times no. With the code of laws in hand, Doctor Zunni will prove that my Aleph is *inalienable*."

I attempted to reason with him.

"But, isn't the cellar very dark?"

"Really, truth does not penetrate a rebellious understanding. If all the places on earth are in the Aleph, the Aleph must also contain all the illuminations, all the lights, all the sources of light."

"I will go and see it at once."

I hung up, before he could issue a prohibition. The knowledge of one fact is enough to allow one to perceive at once a whole series of confirming traits, previously unsuspected. I was astonished not to have understood until that moment that Carlos Argentino was a madman. All the Viterbos, for that matter . . . Beatriz (I often say so myself) was a woman, a girl, of an almost implacable clairvoyance, but there was about her a negligence, a distraction, a disdain, a real cruelty, which perhaps called for a pathological explanation. The madness of Carlos Argentino filled me with malicious felicity; in our innermost beings, we had always detested each other.

In Calle Garay, the serving woman asked me if I would be kind enough to wait. The child was, as always, in the cellar, developing photographs. Next to the flower vase without a single flower in it, atop the useless piano, there smiled (more timeless than anachronic) the great portrait of Beatriz, in dull colors. No one could see us; in an access of tender despair I went up close and told her:

"Beatriz, Beatriz Elena, Beatriz Elena Viterbo, beloved Beatriz, Beatriz lost forever, it's me, Borges."

A little later Carlos came in. He spoke with a certain dryness. I understood that he was incapable of thinking of anything but the loss of the Aleph.

"A glass of the pseudo-cognac," he ordered, "and then you can duck into the cellar. As you already know, the dorsal decubitus is imperative. And so are darkness, immobility, and a certain ocular accommodation. You lie down on the tile floor and fix your eyes on the nineteenth step of the pertinent stairs. I leave, lower the trap door, and you're alone. Quite likely—it should be easy!—some rodent will scare you! In a few minutes you will see the Aleph. The microcosm of alchemists and cabalists, our proverbial concrete friend, the *multum in parvo*!"

Once we were in the dining room he added:

"Of course if you don't see it, your incapacity in no way invalidates my testimony. . . . Now, down with you. Very shortly you will be able to engage in a dialogue with *all* of the images of Beatriz."

I rapidly descended, tired of his insubstantial words. The cellar, barely wider than the stairs, had much of a well about it. I gazed about in search of the trunk of which Carlos Argentino had spoken. Some cases with bottles in them and some canvas bags cluttered one corner. Carlos picked up one of the bags, folded it in half and placed it exactly in a precise spot.

"A humble pillow," he explained, "but if I raise it one centimeter, you won't see a thing, and you'll be left abashed and ashamed. Stretch your bulk out on the floor and count off nineteen steps."

I complied with his ridiculous requisites; and at last he went away. Carefully he closed the trap door; the darkness, despite a crevice which I discovered later, seemed total. And suddenly I realized the danger I ran: I had allowed myself to be buried by a madman, after having drunk some poison! Behind the transparent bravado of Carlos was the intimate terror that I would not see the prodigy; to defend his delirium, to avoid knowing that he was mad, Carlos *had to kill me*. A confused malaise swept over me; I attempted to attribute it to my rigid posture rather than to the operation of a narcotic. I closed my eyes; opened them. Then I saw the Aleph.

I arrive, now, at the ineffable center of my story. And here begins my despair as a writer. All language is an alphabet of symbols whose use presupposes a past shared by all the other interlocutors. How, then, transmit to others the infinite Aleph, which my fearful mind scarcely encompasses? The mystics, in similar situations, are lavish with emblems: to signify the divinity, a Persian speaks of a bird that in some way is all birds; Alanus de Insulis speaks of a sphere whose center is everywhere and whose circumference is nowhere; Ezekiel, of an angel with four faces who looks simultaneously to the Orient and the Occident, to the North and the South. (Not vainly do I recall these inconceivable analogies; they bear some relation to the Aleph.) Perhaps the gods would not be against my finding an equivalent image, but then this report would be contaminated with literature, with falsehood. For the rest, the central problem is unsolvable: the enumeration, even if only partial, of an infinite complex. In that gigantic instant I saw millions of delightful and atrocious acts; none astonished me more than the fact that all of them together occupied the same point, without superposition and without transparency. What my eyes saw was simultaneous: what I shall transcribe is successive, because language is successive. Nevertheless, I shall cull something of it all.

In the lower part of the step, toward the right, I saw a small iridescent sphere, of almost intolerable brilliance. At first I thought it rotary; then I understood that this movement was an illusion produced by the vertiginous sights it enclosed. The Aleph's diameter must have been about two or three centimeters, but Cosmic Space was in it, without diminution of size. Each object (the mirror's glass, for instance) was infinite objects, for I clearly saw it from all points in the universe. I saw the heavy-laden sea; I saw the dawn and the dusk; I saw the multitudes of America; I saw a silver-plated cobweb at the center of a black pyramid; I saw a tattered labyrinth (it was London); I saw interminable eyes nearby looking at me as if in a mirror; I saw all the mirrors in the planet and none reflected me; in an inner patio in the Calle Soler I saw the same paving tile I had seen thirty years before in the entranceway to a house in the town of Fray Bentos; I saw clusters of grapes, snow, tobacco, veins of metal, steam; I saw convex equatorial deserts and every grain of sand in them; I saw a woman at Inverness whom I shall not forget: I saw her violent switch of hair, her proud body, the cancer in her breast; I saw a circle of dry land on a sidewalk where formerly there had been a tree; I saw a villa in Adrogué; I saw a copy of the first English version of Pliny, by Philemon Holland, and saw simultaneously every letter on every page (as a boy I used to marvel that the letters in a closed book did not get mixed up and lost in the course of a night); I saw night and day contemporaneously; I saw a sunset in Querétaro which seemed to reflect the color of a rose in Bengal; I saw my bedroom with nobody in it; I saw in a study in Alkmaar a terraqueous globe between two mirrors which multiplied it without end; I saw horses with swirling manes on a beach by the Caspian Sea at dawn; I saw the delicate bone structure of a hand; I saw the survivors of a battle sending out post cards; I saw a deck of Spanish playing cards in a shopwindow in Mirzapur; I saw the oblique shadows of some ferns on the floor of a hothouse; I saw tigers, emboli, bison, ground swells, and armies; I saw all the ants on earth; I saw a Persian astrolabe; in a desk drawer I saw (the writing made me tremble) obscene, incredible, precise letters, which Beatriz had written Carlos Argentino; I saw an adored monument in La Chacarita cemetery; I saw the atrocious relic of what deliciously had been Beatriz Viterbo; I saw the circulation of my obscure blood; I saw the gearing of love and the modifications of death; I saw the Aleph from all points; I saw the earth in the Aleph and in the earth the Aleph once more and the earth in the Aleph; I saw my face and my viscera; I saw your face and felt vertigo and cried because my eyes had seen that conjectural and secret object whose name men usurp but which no man has gazed on: the inconceivable universe.

I felt infinite veneration, infinite compassion.

"You must be good and dizzy from peering into things that don't concern you," cried a hateful, jovial voice. "Even if you rack your brains, you won't be able to pay me back in a century for this revelation. What a formidable observatory, eh, Borges!"

Carlos Argentino's feet occupied the highest step. In the half-light I managed to get up and to stammer:

"Formidable, yes, formidable."

The indifference in the sound of my voice surprised me. Anxiously Carlos Argentino insisted:

"You saw it all, in colors?"

It was at that instant that I conceived my revenge. Benevolently, with obvious pity, nervous, evasive, I thanked Carlos Argentino for the hospitality of his cellar and urged him to take advantage of the demolition of his house to get far away from the pernicious capital, which is easy on no one, believe me, on no one! I refused, with suave energy, to discuss the Aleph; I embraced him on leaving, and repeated that the country and its quiet are two grand doctors.

In the street, on the Constitución stairs, in the subway, all the faces struck me as familiar. I feared that not a single thing was left to cause me surprise; I was afraid I would never be quit of the impression that I had "returned." Happily, at the end of a few nights of insomnia, forgetfulness worked in me again.

P.S. March 1, 1943

Six months after the demolition of the building in Calle Garay, Procusto Publishers did not take fright at the length of Argentino's considerable poem and launched upon the reading public a selection of "Argentino Extracts." It is almost needless to repeat what happened: Carlos Argentino Daneri received Second Prize, of the National Prizes for Literature.* First Prize was awarded to Doctor Aita; Third, to Doctor Mario Bonfanti; incredibly, my book *The Cards of the Cardsharp* did not get a single vote. Once again incomprehension and envy won the day! For a long time now I have not been able to see Daneri; the daily press says he will soon give us another volume. His fortunate pen (no longer benumbed by the Aleph) has been consecrated to versifying the epitomes of Doctor Acevedo Díaz.

---

* "I received your pained congratulations," he wrote me. "You huff and puff with envy, my lamentable friend, but you must confess— though you choke!—that this time I was able to crown my bonnet with the reddest of feathers, to put in my turban the *caliph* of rubies."

I would like to add two further observations: one, on the
nature of the Aleph; the other, on its name. As is well
known, the latter is the name of the first letter of the alphabet of the sacred language. Its application to the cycle of
my story does not appear mere chance. For the cabala, this
letter signifies the En-Sof, the limitless and pure divinity;
it has also been said that it has the form of a man who
points out heaven and earth, to indicate that the inferior
world is the mirror and map of the superior; for the *Men-
genlehre*, it is the symbol of transfinite numbers, in which
the whole is no greater than any of its parts. I wanted to
know: Had Carlos Argentino chosen this name, or had he
read it, *applied to another point where all points converge,*
in some one of the innumerable texts revealed to him by
the Aleph in his house? Incredible as it may seem, I believe
there is (or was) another Aleph, I believe that the Aleph
in the Calle Garay was a false Aleph.

Here are my reasons. Toward 1867, Captain Burton held
the office of British Consul in Brazil. In July, 1942, Pedro
Henríquez Ureña discovered, in a library at Santos, a
manuscript by Burton dealing with the mirror which the
Orient attributes to Iskandar Zu al-Karnayn, or Alexander
Bicornis of Macedonia. In its glass the entire world was
reflected. Burton mentions other artifices of like kind: the
septuple goblet of Kai Josru; the mirror which Tarik Ben-
zeyad found in a tower (*The Thousand and One Nights,*
272); the mirror which Lucian of Samosata was able to
examine on the moon (*True History,* I, 26); the diaphanous
spear which the first book of Capella's *Satyricon* attributes
to Jupiter; the universal mirror of Merlin, "round and hollow . . . and seemd a world of glas" (*The Faerie Queene,*
III, 2, 19). And he adds these curious words: "But the
former (besides the defect of not existing) are mere instru-
ments of optics. The Faithful who attend the Mosque of
Amr, in Cairo, know very well that the universe is in the

interior of one of the stone columns surrounding the central courtyard. . . . No one, of course, can see it, but those who put their ears to the surface claim to hear, within a short time, its workaday rumor. . . . The mosque dates from the seventh century; the columns come from other, pre-Islamic, temples, for as ibn-Khaldûn has written: '*In republics founded by nomads, the assistance of foreigners is indispensable in all that concerns masonry.*' "

Does that Aleph exist in the innermost recess of a stone? Did I see it when I saw all things, and have I forgotten it? Our minds are porous with forgetfulness; I myself am falsifying and losing, through the tragic erosion of the years, the features of Beatriz.

—*Translated by* Anthony Kerrigan

THE CYCLICAL NIGHT

To Sylvina Bullrich

They knew it, the fervent pupils of Pythagoras:
that stars and men revolve in a cycle;
the fateful atoms will bring back the vital
gold Aphrodite, Thebans and agoras.

In future epochs, the centaur will oppress
with solid, uncleft hoof the breast of the Lapith;
when Rome is dust, the Minotaur will groan
once more in the endless dark of its stinking palace.

Every sleepless night will come back in minute
detail. This writing hand will be born from the same
womb; and bitter armies will contrive their doom.
(The philologist Nietzsche made this very point.)

I do not know if we will recur in a second
cycle, like numbers in a repeating fraction;
but I know that a vague Pythagorean rotation
night after night leaves me on some ground

in the suburbs of the world. A remote spot
which might be either north or east or south,
but always with these things—a crumbled path,
a miraculous wall, a fig tree giving shade.

This, here, is Buenos Aires. Time which brings
to men either love or money, now leaves to me
no more than this withered rose, this empty tracery
of streets with names from the past recurring

155

out of my blood: Laprida, Cabrera, Soler, Suárez . . .
names in which secret bugle calls are sounding,
the republics, the horses and the mornings,
glorious victories and dead soldiers.

Ruined squares at night with no one there
are the vast patios of a crumbled palace,
and the single-minded streets implying Space.
They are corridors out of dreams and nameless fear.

It returns, the concave dark of Anaxagoràs;
in my human flesh, eternity keeps recurring,
and an endless poem, remembered or still in the writing . . .
"They knew it, the fervent pupils of Pythagoras . . ."

—*Translated by* Alastair Reid

ALLUSION TO A GHOST OF THE EIGHTEEN-NINETIES

Nothing. Just Muraña's knife.
Only the truncated story on a gray afternoon.
I don't know why this assassin I never saw
Walks with me at twilight.
Palermo was lower down. The yellow
Prison wall loomed above
The suburbs and the quarter. Through that wild
Part walked Muraña, the sordid Knife.
The Knife. His face has been erased
And all I can recall of that austere mercenary,
Whose craft was courage,
Is a shadow and the flash of steel.
May time, which blurs out marble,
Keep sharp this name: Juan Muraña.

—*Translated by* ANTHONY KERRIGAN

THE TANGO*

"Where are they now?" elegies ask
About those who *are* no longer, as if there were
A region where Yesterday could be
Today, the Still and Not Yet.

Where (I echo) can that malevolence be,
The malignity founded, in dusty dirt
Lanes or in lost towns,
By the sect of defiance and the knife?

Where are they now, those who passed on,
Leaving an episode to Epic,
A fable to Time, men who knifed each other
Without hate or lucre or passion in love?

I look for them in legend, in the final
Ember that like a vague rose
Holds something of that brave crew,
Of men named Corrales or Balvanera.

What obscure alleyways or wasteland
Of heaven is darkened by the hard
Shade of the man who was shadow,
Muraña, that Knife of Palermo?

Where the deadly Iberra (may the saints
forgive him!) who killed his brother
On a railroad overpass, because the other's
Dead were more, and thus he evened the score?

---

* *Tango:* An excellent entry on this Argentine dance par excellence is
to be found in the *Glossaire Argentine* compiled by Juan Montalban for
the exhaustive Borges issue of *L'Herne* (Paris, 1964). *Palermo:* A section of Buenos Aires, named after the church of San Benito de Palermo,
the gift of a Sicilian of the same name. *Milonga:* A descendant of the
habanera and ancestor to the tango.—*Editor's note.*

A mythology of knife thrusts
Slowly dying in oblivion:
A *chanson de geste* lost
In sordid police reports.

There is another ember, another burning rose
In the ash that keeps them whole:
And there the haughty knifers live on
And the silent dagger's bulk:

Though the factious dagger or that other dagger,
Time, sink them in the mire,
Today, beyond time and misshapen
Death, those dead men live on in the tango.

They are in the music, in the strings
Of an obstinate and elaborate guitar
Which weaves a fiesta and the innocence
Of courage into a fortuitous *milonga*.

The yellow carrousel of horse and lion
Whirls in the hollow while I hear the echo
Of those tangos of Arolas and Greco
I watched danced on the pavement

On an instant that today stands out alone,
Without before or after, against oblivion,
And has the taste of everything lost,
Everything lost and recovered.

There is nostalgia in every chord:
The other patio and the half-seen vine.
(The South, behind suspicious walls,
Keeps a knife and a guitar.)

This burst of sound, the tango, this
Wantonness defies the routine years:
Made of time and dust, man lasts
Less long than the libidinous melody,

Which is only time. The tango spawns a turbid
Unreal past in certain measure true:
An impossible recollection of having died
Fighting, on some corner of a suburb.

—Translated by ANTHONY KERRIGAN

BIOGRAPHY OF TADEO ISIDORO CRUZ (1829-1874)

> I'm looking for the face I had
> Before the world was made.
>
> —Yeats, *A Woman Young and Old*.

On the sixth of February, 1829, the irregular troops beating their way north to join the divisions under command of López, already prey to harassment by Lavalle, made a halt at a hacienda whose name was unknown to them, three or four leagues from the Pergamino. Toward dawn, one of the men was victim of an obstinate nightmare: in the depths of a shed's darkness his confused cry awoke the woman who was sleeping with him. Nobody knows what he dreamt, for on the next day, at four o'clock, the irregulars were routed by the cavalry under Suárez and the chase lasted for nine leagues, as far as the tall grass, where the fields had already gone dark, and the man perished in a ditch, his skull sliced open by a saber from the Peruvian and Brazilian wars. The woman was called Isidora Cruz. The son she bore was christened Tadeo Isidoro.

It is not my purpose to repeat his story. Of the days and nights which compose it only one night is of interest to me; of the rest I shall not relate any more than what is indispensable to make that one night understandable. The adventure is recorded in a notable book; that is to say, in a book whose matter may be "all things to all men" (I Corinthians 9:22), for it is capable of almost inexhaustible repetitions, versions and perversions. Those who have glossed the history of Tadeo Isidoro—and they are legion—have emphasized the influence of the plains upon the formation of his nature, but gauchos identical to him have been born and have died upon the wild banks of the Paraná River and on the eastern ranges. He did, true enough, live in a world of monotonous barbarity. When he died, in 1874, of the black pox, he had never seen a mountain nor a gas spigot nor a mill. Nor did he ever see a city. In 1849 he went to Buenos Aires with a drove of cattle from the establishment of Francisco Xavier Acevedo; the drovers went into the city to empty their money belts; Cruz, mistrustful, did not go beyond an inn in the stockyards. He spent many days there, taciturn, sleeping on the ground, drinking maté tea, getting up at dawn and going to bed at the hour of afternoon prayer. He understood (beyond the range of words or even of the mind) that the city had nothing to do with him. One of the *peones*, drunk, made fun of him. Cruz made no reply, but during the nights of the return journey, the *peón* repeated his taunts around the campfire, and then Cruz (who up until then had not shown any rancor, or even annoyance) laid him out with a single knife thrust. In his subsequent flight, the fugitive took refuge in a marshland. Some nights later, the cry of a crested screamer warned him that the police had encircled him. He tested his knife on a shrub; to give him greater freedom if he should have to fight dismounted, he slipped off his spurs. He chose to defend himself rather than surrender. He was wounded on the forearm, the shoulder, the left hand; he severely wounded the fiercest of his opponents; when the blood began to run between his fingers, he fought with greater courage than ever. Toward dawn, as he grew dizzy with loss of blood, he was disarmed. In those days, the army performed a penal function: Cruz was sent off to serve in a small outpost on the northern frontier. He took part in the civil wars as a private; sometimes he fought for his native province, sometimes against. On the twenty-third of January, 1856, at Lagunas de Cardoso, he was one of the thirty Christians who, under the command of Sergeant Major Eusebio Laprida, fought two hundred Indians. In this action he received a lance wound.

There are great gaps in his obscure and brave story. We know that in about 1868 he was again in the region of the Pergamino: married or living in concubinage, he was the father of a child and the proprietor of a bit of field. In 1869 he was made sergeant of the rural police. He had now rectified the past. At that time he must have considered himself happy, though profoundly he was not. (A luminous, fundamental night, still hidden in the future, awaited him: the night on which he saw his own face at last, the night on which he heard at last his name. In all truth, that one night exhausts his story; or rather, one instant in that night, one act in that night, for acts are our symbol.) Any destiny at all, however long and complicated, in reality consists *of a single moment:* the moment in which a man once and for all knows who he is. It is said that Alexander of Macedonia saw his ironbound future reflected in the fabulous history of Achilles; Charles XII of Sweden saw his in that of Alexander. This knowledge was not given in a book to Tadeo Isidoro Cruz, who did not know how to read; he saw himself revealed in a hand-to-hand combat between horsemen and he saw himself in one man. Events transpired in the following manner:

In the last days of June, 1870, he received orders to arrest an outlaw who owed two deaths to justice. The outlaw was a deserter from the southern frontier forces under Colonel Benito Machado; during a drunken spree he had done in a mulatto in a brothel; in another such episode, he had killed a resident of the district of Rojas; the report on him added that he came from Laguna Colorada. It was at this place that the irregulars had gathered forty years earlier before embarking on the misadventure which had turned them into feed for the crows and bones for the dogs; it was from here that Manuel Mesa had come, to be finally executed in the Plaza de la Victoria while the drums rolled to drown out the sound of his wrath; it was from here had come the unknown who had engendered Cruz and died in a ditch, his skull sliced open by a saber from the battles of Peru and Brazil. Cruz had forgotten that name; it was with a slight but inexplicable disquiet that he recognized it now. . . .

The criminal, closely pursued by the soldiers, wove on horseback a long and devious labyrinth by his comings and goings; nevertheless, on the night of July 12, the soldiers cornered him. He had taken refuge in a field of tall grass. The darkness was almost indecipherable. Cruz and his men, wary and on foot, advanced toward the brush in whose tremulous depths the secret man was lurking or sleeping. A crested screamer cried out. Tadeo Isidoro Cruz had the feeling that he had already lived this moment. The fugitive emerged from his lair to fight. Cruz descried him, a terrible sight: the overgrown mane of hair and the gray beard seemed to consume his face. I can not, for a notorious reason, give the details of the fight. Let it suffice to recall that the deserter badly wounded or killed several of Cruz's men. Cruz himself, as he fought in the obscurity (while his body fought in the obscurity), began to understand. He understood that one destiny is no better than another, but that every man should revere the destiny he bears within him. He understood that the other cavalrymen and his own uniform were now a burden to him. He understood his intimate destiny, that of wolf and not of gregarious dog. He understood that the other man was himself. The dawn broke over the enormous plain. Cruz threw down his kepi, cried out that he would not be party to the crime of killing a brave man, and began to fight the soldiers alongside the deserter Martín Fierro.*

—*Translated by* ANTHONY KERRIGAN

---

* The non-Argentine reader may lose some of the emotional significance of this episode, unless he knows that Martín Fierro is the heroic ("*béatifié*," says Montalban, in his "Glossaire Argentin," Borges Cahier, *L'Herne*) archetype of the gaucho, and hero of the epic poem of the same name.—*Editor's note.*

THE END*

Lying prone, Recabarren half-opened his eyes and saw the
slanting rattan ceiling. The thrumming of a guitar reached
him from the other room; the invisible instrument was a
kind of meager labyrinth infinitely winding and unwinding.
. . . Little by little he returned to reality, to the daily details
which now would never change. He gazed without sorrow at
his great useless body, at the poncho of coarse wool wrapped
around his legs. Outside, beyond the barred windows,
stretched the plain and the afternoon. He had been sleeping,
but the sky was still filled with light. Groping about with
his left arm, he finally touched a bronze cowbell hanging
at the foot of the cot. He banged on it two or three times;
from the other side of the door the humble chords continued
to reach him. The guitarist was a Negro who had shown up
one night to display his pretensions as a singer: he had
challenged another stranger to a drawn-out contest of singing to guitar accompaniment. Bested, he nevertheless continued to haunt the general store, as if waiting for someone.
He passed the hours playing on his guitar, but he no longer
ventured to sing. Perhaps his defeat had embittered him.
The other customers had grown accustomed to this inoffensive player. Recabarren, the shopowner, would never forget the songs of the guitar contest: the next day, as he
adjusted a load of maté upon a mule's back, his right side

---

* This account of a knife fight with Martín Fierro, the Argentine
gaucho of José Hernández' great folk poem, takes up the story of Fierro
where the popular poem leaves off. A singing encounter, or challenge,
with a black man (one of ten brothers, the eldest of whom has been
killed) occurs toward the end of the poem. A fight is at that time
averted. Borges here gives us the account of a subsequent meeting. (And
see Prologue to *Artifices*, in the volume *Ficciones:* Grove Press, 1962.)—
Editor's note.

had suddenly died and he had lost his power of speech. By dint of taking pity on the misfortunes of the heroes of novels we come to take too much pity on our own misfortunes; not so the enduring Recabarren, who accepted his paralysis as he had previously accepted the rude solitude of America. Habituated to living in the present, like the animals, he gazed now at the sky and considered how the crimson circle around the moon presaged rain.

A boy with Indian features (one of his sons, perhaps) half-opened the door. Recabarren asked him with his eyes if there were anyone in the shop. The boy, taciturn, indicated by terse signs that there was no one. (The Negro, of course, did not count.) The prostrate man was left alone. One hand played briefly with the cowbell, as if he were wielding some power.

Beneath the final sun of the day, the plain seemed almost abstract, as if seen in a dream. A point shimmered on the horizon, and then grew until it became a horseman, who came, or seemed to come, toward the building. Recabarren saw the wide-brimmed hat, the long, dark poncho, the dappled horse, but not the man's face; at length the rider tightened the reins and cut down the gallop, approaching at a trot. Some two hundred yards away, he turned sharply. Recabarren could no longer see him, but he heard him speak, dismount, tie the horse to the paling, and enter the shop with a firm step.

Without raising his eyes from his instrument, where he seemed to be searching for something, the Negro said gently:

"I was sure, *señor,* that I could count on you."

The other man replied with a harsh voice:

"And I on you, colored man. I made you wait many days, but here I am."

There was a silence. At length the Negro responded:

"I'm getting used to waiting. I've waited seven years."

Without haste the other explained:

"I went longer than seven years without seeing my children. I saw them that day, but I didn't want to seem like a man always fighting."

"I realize that. I understand what you say," said the Negro. "I trust you left them in good health."

The stranger, who had taken a seat at the bar, laughed a deep laugh. He asked for a rum. He drank with relish, but did not drain it down.

"I gave them some good advice," he declared. "That's never amiss, and it doesn't cost anything. I told them, among other things, that one man should not shed another man's blood."

A slow chord preceded the Negro's reply:

"You did well. That way they won't be like us."

"At least they won't be like me," said the stranger. And then he added, as if he were ruminating aloud: "Destiny has made me kill, and now, once more, it has put a knife in my hand."

The Negro, as if he had not heard, observed:

"Autumn is making the days grow shorter."

"The light that's left is enough for me," replied the stranger, getting to his feet.

He stood in front of the Negro and said, with weariness:

"Leave off the guitar. Today there's another kind of counterpoint waiting for you."

The two men walked toward the door. As he went out, the Negro murmured:

"Perhaps this time it will go as hard on me as the first time."

The other answered seriously:

"It didn't go hard on you the first time. What happened was that you were anxious for the second try."

They moved away from the houses for a good bit, walking together. One point on the plain was as good as another, and the moon was shining. Suddenly they looked at each other, halted, and the stranger began taking off his spurs. They already had their ponchos wound around their forearms when the Negro said:

"I want to ask you a favor before we tangle. I want you to put all your guts into this meeting, just as you did seven years ago, when you killed my brother."

Perhaps for the first time in the dialogue, Martín Fierro heard the sound of hate. He felt his blood like a goad. They clashed, and the sharp-edged steel marked the Negro's face.

There is an hour of the afternoon when the plain is on the verge of saying something. It never says it, or perhaps it says it infinitely, or perhaps we do not understand it, or we understand it and it is as untranslatable as music. . . . From his cot, Recabarren saw the end. A charge, and the Negro fell back; he lost his footing, feinted toward the other's face, and reached out in a great stab, which penetrated the stranger's chest. Then there was another stab, which the shopowner did not clearly see, and Fierro did not get up. Immobile, the Negro seemed to watch over his enemy's laboring death agony. He wiped his bloodstained knife on the turf and walked back toward the knot of houses slowly, without looking back. His righteous task accomplished, he was nobody. More accurately, he became the stranger: he had no further mission on earth, but he had killed a man.

—*Translated by* Anthony Kerrigan

STORY OF THE WARRIOR
AND THE CAPTIVE

To Ulrike von Kühlmann.

On page 278 of his *La Poesia* (Bari, 1942), Croce, summarizing a Latin text of the historian Paul the Deacon, recounts the fortunes and quotes the epitaph of Droctulft; I was extraordinarily moved, and later I understood why. Droctulft was a Lombard warrior who deserted to the enemy during the siege of Ravenna, and died defending the city he had previously attacked. The Ravennese buried him in a temple and composed an epitaph in which they expressed both their gratitude (*"contempsit caros, dum nos amat ille, parentes"*) and the striking contrast to be found between that barbarian's terrible face and his simplicity and goodness:

> *Terribilis visu facies, sed mente benignus,*
> *Longaque robusto pectores barba fuit!**

Such is the story of Droctulft, a barbarian who died defending Rome, or such, at any rate, is the fragment of his story that Paul the Deacon was able to recover. I do not even know when this took place: whether about the middle of the sixth century, when the Longobardi laid waste the plains of Italy; whether in the eighth century, before the surrender of Ravenna. Let us imagine (since this is not a historical work) the first to be the case.

Let us imagine Droctulft *sub specie aeternitatis*, not the individual Droctulft who was, doubtlessly, like all individ-

---

* Gibbon (*Decline and Fall*, XLV) also transcribes these verses.

uals, unique and unfathomable, but the generic type that tradition (which is a product of oblivion and memory) has made of him and of many others like him. The wars brought him from the banks of the Danube and the Elbe across a dim geography of forests and marshes to Italy, and he perhaps did not know that he was journeying south and that he was warring against the name of Rome. Perhaps he professed Arianism, which holds that the glory of the Son is a reflection of the Father's glory, but it is more suitable to imagine him a worshiper of Earth, of Hertha, whose veiled image went from hut to hut in a cart drawn by cows, or of the gods of war and thunder, rude wooden figures wrapped in homespun clothes and heaped with coins and bangles. He came from the dense forests of the wild boar and the aurochs; he was white, brave, innocent, cruel, loyal to his captain and his tribe but not to the universe. The wars bring him to Ravenna and there he sees something he has never seen, or has not seen . . . in such plenitude. He sees the day and cypresses and marble. He sees a whole that is complex and yet without disorder; he sees a city, an organism composed of statues, temples, gardens, dwellings, stairways, urns, capitals, of regular and open spaces. None of these artifacts (I know) impresses him as beautiful; they move him as we might be moved today by a complex machine of whose purpose we are ignorant but in whose design we can intuit an immortal intelligence. Perhaps it is enough for him to see a single arch, with an incomprehensible inscription in eternal Roman letters. Abruptly, that revelation, the City, blinds him and renews him. He knows that in that city he will be a dog, or a child, and that he will not even begin to understand it, but that it is worth more than his gods and his sworn faith and the German marshes. Droctulft deserts, and goes to fight for Ravenna. He dies, and words he would not have understood are carved on his tomb:

Contempsit caros, dum nos amat ille, parentes,
Hanc patriam reputans esse, Ravenna, suam.

He was not a traitor (traitors do not inspire pious epi-taphs), he was a visionary, a convert. After several genera-tions, the Longobardi who condemned the deserter, did as he had done: they became Italians, Lombards, and perhaps someone of that race—Aldiger—may have engendered those who engendered Alighieri. . . . Many conjectures may be made to explain Droctulft's act; mine is the most economical; if it is not literally true, it is symbolically so.

When I read this story of the warrior in Croce's book, I was moved in an unusual way and had the impression I was recovering, in a different form, something that had been mine. I thought fleetingly of the Mongol horsemen who wanted to turn China into an infinite pasture and then grew old in the cities they had longed to destroy. That was not the memory I sought. I found it at last: it was a tale I had sometimes heard from my English grandmother, who is now dead.

In 1872, my grandfather Borges was commander of the northern and western frontiers of Buenos Aires Province and of the southern frontier of Santa Fe Province. His headquarters were in Junín; beyond that, four or five leagues from one another, the chain of outposts; beyond that, what was then called the pampas and also Tierra Adentro. Now and then, half-astonished, half-mocking, my grandmother spoke of her destiny as an Englishwoman exiled to that end of the earth. She was told she was not the only one, and, months later, an Indian girl who was slowly crossing the plaza was pointed out to her. She was wearing two red blankets and went barefoot; her hair was blond. A soldier told her that another Englishwoman wanted to speak to her. The woman consented, and entered the headquarters fearlessly, though with misgivings. In her coppery face, which was streaked with fierce colors, her eyes were of that wan blue the English call gray. Her body was light, like a deer's; her hands, strong and bony. Coming from the wilderness, the pampas, she seemed to find everything too small for her: the doors, the walls, the furniture.

Perhaps the two women felt for an instant as if they were sisters, here in this incredible land far from their own beloved island. My grandmother said something; the other answered with difficulty, searching for the words and repeating them as if astonished by an ancient savor. She had not spoken her native tongue for fifteen years and it was not easy to take it up again. She said that she was from Yorkshire, that her parents had emigrated to Buenos Aires, that she had lost them in an Indian raid, that the Indians had carried her off, and that now she was the wife of a chieftain to whom she had already given two sons and who was very brave. She said all this in a rustic English interspersed with Auracan and the pampas' dialect. A savage life could be glimpsed behind her tale: the horsehide Indian huts, the fires made of manure, the feasts of scorched meat or of raw entrails, the silent dawn marches; the attacks on the corrals, the yelling and plundering, the naked horsemen charging the haciendas; war, polygamy, stenches, magic. An Englishwoman had lowered herself to this barbarism. Shocked and pitiful, my grandmother urged her not to return, and promised to protect her and to rescue her children. The woman answered that she was happy, and, that night, returned to the wilderness. Francisco Borges died shortly afterward, in the revolution of '74. Perhaps my grandmother was then able to see in that other woman, swept away and transformed by this implacable continent, a monstrous mirror of her own destiny. . . .

The blond Indian woman used to go every year to buy trinkets in the general stores in Junín or Fuerte Lavalle; she did not turn up again after her conversation with my grandmother. Nevertheless, they saw each other once more. My grandmother had gone out hunting; on a ranch, near the sheep-dip, a man was cutting the throat of a sheep. As if in a dream, the Indian woman came by on a horse. She threw herself to the ground and drank the warm blood. I don't know whether she did this because she could no longer act differently or as a challenge and a sign.

Thirteen hundred years and an ocean stretch between the destiny of the captive and the destiny of Droctulft. Today, the two are equally irretrievable. The figure of the barbarian who embraces the cause of Ravenna and the figure of the European woman who chooses the wilderness may seem antithetical. Nevertheless, both were carried away by a secret impulse, an impulse deeper than reason, and both obeyed this impulse they could not have justified. Perhaps the stories I have recounted are a single story. To God, the obverse and reverse of this coin are the same.

—Translated by IRVING FELDMAN

THE CAPTIVE

They tell this story in Junín or in Tapalqué. A boy disappeared after an Indian raid; he was said to have been carried off by the Indians. His parents pressed a futile search for him. After long years a soldier who came from the interior told them of an Indian with sky-blue eyes, who might very well be their son. At last they found this man (the chronicle loses track of the exact circumstances and I don't want to invent what I don't know) and thought they recognized him. The man, formed by the lonely life of the wilds, no longer understood the words of his native language, but let himself be led, indifferent and docile, up to their house. There he stopped, perhaps because the others stopped. He looked at the door, but without understanding. Suddenly, he lowered his head, let out a shout, went down the entrance hall and the two long patios at a run, and burst into the kitchen. Without hesitation he plunged his arm up the blackened fireplace chimney and pulled out a little horn-handle knife he had hidden there as a boy. His eyes shone with joy and his parents wept because they had found their son.

Perhaps other recollections followed this one, but the Indian was not able to live within walls, and one day he went off to look for his wilderness. I wonder what he felt in that vertiginous moment when the past and the present were confused; I would like to know if the lost son was reborn and died in that moment of rapture, or if he managed to recognize, like an infant or a dog at least, his parents and his home.

—*Translated by* ELAINE KERRIGAN

PARADISO XXXI, 108

Diodorus Siculus narrates the story of a dismembered and sundered god, who, as he walks in the twilight or traces a date in his past, never senses that something infinite has been lost.

Mankind has lost a face, an irretrievable face, and everyone would like to be that pilgrim (dreamed of in the empyrean, under the Rose) who sees Veronica's handkerchief in Rome and murmurs with faith: *Jesus Christ, My Lord, True God, this, then, was Your Face?*

There is a stone face on a certain road and an inscription which reads: *The true Portrait of the Holy Face of the God of Jaén.* If we really knew the likeness, we would have the key to the parables and would know if the son of the carpenter was also the Son of God.

Paul saw it in the guise of a light which hurled him to the ground; John, as the sun shining in full force; Teresa of Jesus, oftentimes, as if bathed in a tranquil light, but she was never able to specify the color of the eyes.

We lost those features, in the way a magical number may be lost, a number made up of customary figures; in the same way as an image in a kaleidoscope is lost forever. We may see them, and not know it. The profile of a Jew in the subway may be that of Christ; the hands which give us some coins at a change-window may recall those which some soldiers once nailed to the Cross.

Perhaps some feature of the Crucified Face lurks in every mirror; perhaps the Face died, was effaced, so that God might become everyone.

Who knows whether we may not see it tonight in the labyrinths of dreams and remember nothing tomorrow.

—*Translated by* ANTHONY KERRIGAN

LUKE 23

Gentile or Hebrew or simply one
Whose face has been lost to us in time;
We shall not rescue from oblivion
Now the silent letters of his name.

He knew of mercy what a bandit may
Whom Judea has nailed to a cross.
And we today are at a loss
About the time preceding. That day

At his task of dying crucified,
He heard, amid the crowd's mockery,
That he who was dying at his side
Was a god, and said to him blindly,

Remember me when you inherit
Your kingdom, and the inconceivable voice
That shall judge one day each man's merit
Promised him from the terrible cross

Paradise. Nothing more was said
Until the end came, but history
Shall preserve from death the memory
Of the afternoon on which they died.

Oh friends, the innocence of this friend
Of Jesus, the candor that moved him
From the ignominy of his end
To ask for Heaven and receive it,

Was the very same that so many times
Had hurled him into sin and bloody crimes.

—*Translated by* IRVING FELDMAN

177

THE WITNESS

In a stable lying almost in the shadow of the new stone church, a man with gray eyes and a gray beard, stretched on the ground amidst the animal odors, meekly seeks death like someone seeking sleep. The day, faithful to vast secret laws, continuously displaces and confounds the shadows in the wretched stable. Outside stretch the tilled fields, a deep ditch filled up with dead leaves, and the tracks of a wolf in the black mud where the woods begin. The man sleeps and dreams, forgotten. The bells calling to prayer awake him. In the kingdoms of England, the sound of the bells is already one of the customs of the afternoon, but the man, while still a boy, had seen the face of Woden, had seen holy dread and exultation, had seen the rude wooden idol weighed down with Roman coins and heavy vestments, seen the sacrifice of horses, dogs, and prisoners. Before dawn he would be dead and with him would die, never to return, the last firsthand images of the pagan rites. The world would be poorer when this Saxon was no more.

We may well be astonished by space-filling acts which come to an end when someone dies, and yet something, or an infinite number of things, die in each death—unless there is a universal memory, as the theosophists have conjectured. There was a day in time when the last eyes to see Christ were closed forever. The battle of Junín and the love of Helen died with the death of some one man. What will die with me when I die? What pathetic or frail form will the world lose? Perhaps the voice of Macedonio Fernández, the image of a horse in the vacant space at Serrano and Charcas, a bar of sulfur in the drawer of a mahogany desk?

—*Translated by* ANTHONY KERRIGAN

THE MODESTY OF HISTORY

On the twentieth of September, 1792, Johann Wolfgang von Goethe (who had accompanied the Duke of Weimar to Paris on a military excursion) saw the finest army in Europe inexplicably repulsed at Valmy by some French militia, and he told his disconcerted friends: *At this place and on this day a new epoch in the history of the world begins, and we shall be able to say that we were present at its beginnings*. Ever since that day there has been a plethora of historical dates and days, and one of the tasks of modern governments (most notably in Italy, Germany, and Russia) has been to fabricate or counterfeit them, with the help of previously accumulated propaganda and of persistent publicity. Such "historic" dates, in which the influence of Cecil B. DeMille may be noted, bear less relation to history than to journalism. I have long suspected that history, true history, is far more modest, and that its essential dates may well be, for a long time, secret as well. A Chinese writer of prose has observed that the unicorn, for the very reason that it is so anomalous, will pass unnoticed. Our eyes see what they are accustomed to see. Tacitus did not perceive the Crucifixion, though his book records the event.

I was led to these reflections by a chance phrase which caught my eye as I leafed through a history of Greek literature and which interested me because of its slightly enigmatic nature. Here is the phrase: *He brought in a second actor*. I paused, verified the fact that Aeschylus was the subject of this mysterious action, and that, as is stated in the Fourth Chapter of Aristotle's *Poetics*, he "raised the number of actors from one to two." As we know, the drama was born of the Dionysiac religion; originally, a single actor, the *hypocrite*, made taller by the thick-soled

179

buskin, the cothurnus, dressed in black or purple, his face made larger by a mask, shared the stage with the twelve members of the chorus. The drama was one of the ceremonies of the cult, and, as in all ritual, it ran the risk of some day being invariable. This could have happened, but that one day, five hundred years before the Christian era, the Athenians marveled to see, or were scandalized to see (Victor Hugo surmised the latter), the unannounced appearance of a second actor. On that day in some remote spring, in that honey-colored theater, what did those Athenians think, what did they feel? Perhaps neither stupor nor consternation; perhaps only the beginnings of surprise. From Cicero's *Tusculanae Disputationes* we know that Aeschylus entered the Pythagorean order, but we shall never know whether or not he foresaw, even though only imperfectly, the significance of the progressive passage from one to two, from unity to plurality, and thus on to infinity. Along with the second actor came dialogue and the indefinite possibilities of the reaction of some characters upon others. A prophetic spectator would have seen that multitudes of future apparitions accompanied the second actor: Hamlet and Faust and Sigismundo and Macbeth and Peer Gynt, and others whom our eyes can not yet discern.

In the course of my reading I discovered another historical date. It happened in Iceland, in the thirteenth century of our era: in 1225, let us say. The historian and polygraph Snorri Sturlason, at his country house in Borgarfjord, wrote down, for the enlightenment of future generations, the details of the last exploit of the famous king Harald Sigurdarson, called the Implacable (Hardrada), who had previously fought in Byzantium, Italy, and Africa. Now Tostig, brother to the Saxon king of England, Harold Son of Godwin (Harold II), coveted power and had gained the support of Harald Sigurdarson. They landed at the head of a Norwegian army on the east coast of England and reduced the fortress of Jorvik (York). South of Jorvik, they were met by the Saxon army. After relating this sequence of events, Snorri continues.

> Twenty horsemen approached the ranks of the invader. The men, and also the horses, were dressed in mail. One of the horsemen shouted:
> "Is Earl Tostig there?"
> "I don't deny being here," said the Earl.
> "If you really are Tostig," said the horseman, "I've come to tell you that your brother offers you his pardon and a third part of the kingdom."
> "If I accept," said Tostig, "what will the King give Harald Sigurdarson?"
> "He has not forgotten him," answered the horseman. "He'll give him six feet of English earth and, since he is so tall, an extra foot besides."
> "In that case," said Tostig, "tell your king that we will fight to the death."
> The horsemen rode away. Pensively Harald Sigurdarson asked:
> "Who was that gentleman who spoke so well?"
> "Harold Son of Godwin."

Other chapters recount how before the sun set that day, the Norwegian army was defeated. Harald Sigurdarson died in battle, and so did the Earl (*Heimskringla*, X, 92).

There is a certain flavor, a savor which our time (weary, perhaps, with the artless imitations by the professionals of patriotism) does not perceive without some suspicion: the elementary savor of heroism. I am assured that the *Poem of the Cid* has this savor; I have tasted it, unmistakably, in some verses of the *Aeneid* ("Son, from me learn courage and true constancy; from others, success."), in the Anglo-Saxon ballad of Maldon ("My people will pay the tribute with lances and old swords."), in the *Chanson de Roland*, in Victor Hugo, in Whitman, and in

Faulkner ("lavender, stronger than the odor of horses and of courage"), in the *Epitaph on an Army of Mercenaries* of Housman, and in the "six feet of English earth" of the *Heimskringla*. Behind the apparently simple statement of the historian lies a delicate psychical play. Harold pretends not to recognize his brother, so that the latter in his turn may realize that he should not recognize him either; Tostig does not betray him, but neither will he betray his ally; Harold, prepared to pardon his brother, but not to tolerate the interference of the King of Norway, proceeds in a very understandable manner. I say nothing of the verbal adroitness of his reply: the gift of one third of the kingdom, the gift of six feet of earth.*

There is only one thing more admirable than the admirable reply of the Saxon king: the fact that it was an Icelander, a man of the blood of the defeated, who perpetuated it. It is as if a Carthaginian had bequeathed us the memory of Regulus and his defiance. With good reason Saxo Grammaticus writes in his *Gesta Danorum:* "The men of Thule (Iceland) take pleasure in learning and recording the history of all peoples and they consider it just as glorious to proclaim alien merits as to publish their own."

It was not so much the day on which the Saxon spoke his words, but rather the day on which an enemy perpetuated them that constitutes a historic date. It was a prophetic date, as well, prophetic of something that lies in the future: the overlooking of blood and nationality, the solidarity of the human race. Harold's offer owes its merit to the concept of fatherland; Snorri, by virtue of his recording it, surpasses and transcends it.

I recall another tribute to an enemy in the final chapters of Lawrence's *Seven Pillars of Wisdom*. Lawrence praises

---

* Carlyle, in his *Early Kings of Norway,* spoils the economy of the phrase with an unfortunate addition, when, to the "six feet of English earth" he adds "for a grave."

the courage of a German detachment, and writes these words: "Then, for the first time in that campaign, I was proud of the men who had killed my brothers." And he adds: "They were glorious."

—*Translated by* ANTHONY KERRIGAN

THE SECRET MIRACLE

> And God made him die during the
> course of a hundred years and then
> He revived him and said:
> "How long have you been here?"
> "A day, or part of a day," he
> replied.
>
> —*The Koran*, II 261

On the night of March 14, 1939, in an apartment on the
Zelternergasse in Prague, Jaromir Hladík, author of the
unfinished tragedy *The Enemies*, of a *Vindication of Eternity*, and of an inquiry into the indirect Jewish sources of
Jakob Boehme, dreamt a long-drawn-out chess game. The
antagonists were not two individuals, but two illustrious
families. The contest had begun many centuries before.
No one could any longer describe the forgotten prize, but
it was rumored that it was enormous and perhaps infinite.
The pieces and the chessboard were set up in a secret
tower. Jaromir (in his dream) was the first-born of one of
the contending families. The hour for the next move, which
could not be postponed, struck on all the clocks. The
dreamer ran across the sands of a rainy desert—and he
could not remember the chessmen or the rules of chess. At
this point he awoke. The din of the rain and the clangor of
the terrible clocks ceased. A measured unison, sundered
by voices of command, arose from the Zelternergasse. Day
had dawned, and the armored vanguards of the Third Reich
were entering Prague.

On the nineteenth, the authorities received an accusation
against Jaromir Hladík; on the same day, at dusk, he was

arrested. He was taken to a barracks, aseptic and white, on the opposite bank of the Moldau. He was unable to refute a single one of the charges made by the Gestapo: his maternal surname was Jaroslavski, his blood was Jewish, his study of Boehme was Judaizing, his signature had helped to swell the final census of those protesting the *Anschluss*. In 1928, he had translated the *Sepher Yezirah* for the publishing house of Hermann Barsdorf; the effusive catalogue issued by this firm had exaggerated, for commercial reasons, the translator's renown; this catalogue was leafed through by Julius Rothe, one of the officials in whose hands lay Hladík's fate. The man does not exist who, outside his own specialty, is not credulous: two or three adjectives in Gothic script sufficed to convince Julius Rothe of Hladík's preeminence, and of the need for the death penalty, *pour encourager les autres*. The execution was set for the twenty-ninth of March, at nine in the morning. This delay (whose importance the reader will appreciate later) was due to a desire on the part of the authorities to act slowly and impersonally, in the manner of planets or vegetables.

Hladík's first reaction was simply one of horror. He was sure he would not have been terrified by the gallows, the block, or the knife; but to die before a firing squad was unbearable. In vain he repeated to himself that the pure and general act of dying, not the concrete circumstances, was the dreadful fact. He did not grow weary of imagining these circumstances: he absurdly tried to exhaust all the variations. He infinitely anticipated the process, from the sleepless dawn to the mysterious discharge of the rifles. Before the day set by Julius Rothe, he died hundreds of deaths, in courtyards whose shapes and angles defied geometry, shot down by changeable soldiers whose number varied and who sometimes put an end to him from close up and sometimes from far away. He faced these imaginary executions with true terror (perhaps with true courage). Each simulacrum lasted a few seconds. Once the circle was closed, Jaromir returned interminably to the tremulous eve of his death. Then he would reflect that reality does not tend to coincide with forecasts about it. With perverse logic he inferred that to foresee a circumstantial detail is to prevent its happening. Faithful to this feeble magic, he would invent, *so that they might not happen,* the most atrocious particulars. Naturally, he finished by fearing that these particulars were prophetic. During his wretched nights he strove to hold fast somehow to the fugitive substance of time. He knew that time was precipitating itself toward the dawn of the twenty-ninth. He reasoned aloud: *I am now in the night of the twenty-second. While this night lasts (and for six more nights to come) I am invulnerable, immortal.* His nights of sleep seemed to him deep, dark pools into which he might submerge. Sometimes he yearned impatiently for the firing squad's definitive volley, which would redeem him, for better or for worse, from the vain compulsion of his imagination. On the twenty-eighth, as the final sunset reverberated across the high barred windows, he was distracted from all these abject considerations by thought of his drama, *The Enemies.*

Hladík was past forty. Apart from a few friendships and many habits, the problematic practice of literature constituted his life. Like every writer, he measured the virtues of other writers by their performance, and asked that they measure him by what he conjectured or planned. All of the books he had published merely moved him to a complex repentance. His investigation of the work of Boehme, of Ibn Ezra, and of Fludd was essentially a product of mere application; his translation of the *Sepher Yezirah* was characterized by negligence, fatigue, and conjecture. He judged his *Vindication of Eternity* to be perhaps less deficient: the first volume is a history of the diverse eternities devised by man, from the immutable Being of Parmenides to the alterable past of Hinton; the second volume denies (with Francis Bradley) that all the events in the universe make up a temporal series. He argues that the number of experiences possible to man is not infinite, and that a single "repetition" suffices to demonstrate that time is a fallacy. . . . Unfortunately, the arguments that demonstrate this fallacy are not any less fallacious. Hladík was in the habit of running through these arguments with a certain disdainful perplexity. He had also written a series of expressionist poems; these, to the discomfiture of the author, were included in an anthology in 1924, and there was no anthology of later date which did not inherit them. Hladík was anxious to redeem himself from his equivocal and languid past with his verse drama, *The Enemies*. (He favored the verse form in the theater because it prevents the spectators from forgetting unreality, which is the necessary condition of art.)

This opus preserved the dramatic unities (time, place, and action). It transpires in Hradcany, in the library of the Baron Roemerstadt, on one of the last evenings of the nineteenth century. In the first scene of the first act, a stranger pays a visit to Roemerstadt. (A clock strikes seven, the vehemence of a setting sun glorifies the window panes, the air transmits familiar and impassioned Hungarian music.) This visit is followed by others; Roemerstadt does not know the people who come to importune him, but he has the uncomfortable impression that he has seen them before: perhaps in a dream. All the visitors fawn upon him, but it is obvious—first to the spectators of the drama, and then to the Baron himself—that they are secret enemies, sworn to ruin him. Roemerstadt manages to outwit, or evade, their complex intrigues. In the course of the dialogue, mention is made of his betrothed, Julia de Weidenau, and of a certain Jaroslav Kubin, who at one time had been her suitor. Kubin has now lost his mind and thinks he is Roemerstadt. . . . The dangers multiply. Roemerstadt, at the end of the second act, is forced to kill one of the conspirators. The third and final act begins. The incongruities gradually mount up: actors who seemed to have been discarded from the play reappear; the man who had been killed by Roemerstadt returns, for an instant. Someone notes that the time of day has not advanced: the clock strikes seven, the western sun reverberates in the high windowpanes, impassioned Hungarian music is carried on the air. The first speaker in the play reappears and repeats the words he had spoken in the first scene of the first act. Roemerstadt addresses him without the least surprise. The spectator understands that Roemerstadt is the wretched Jaroslav Kubin. The drama has never taken place: it is the circular delirium which Kubin unendingly lives and relives.

Hladík had never asked himself whether this tragicomedy of errors was preposterous or admirable, deliberate or casual. Such a plot, he intuited, was the most appropriate invention to conceal his defects and to manifest his strong points, and it embodied the possibility of redeeming (symbolically) the fundamental meaning of his life. He had already completed the first act and a scene or two of the third. The metrical nature of the work allowed him to go over it continually, rectifying the hexameters, without recourse to the manuscript. He thought of the two acts still to do, and of his coming death. In the darkness, he addressed himself to God. *If I exist at all, if I am not one of Your repetitions and errata, I exist as the author of* The Enemies. *In order to bring this drama, which may serve to justify me, to justify You, I need one more year. Grant me that year, You to whom belong the centuries and all time.* It was the last, the most atrocious night, but ten minutes later sleep swept over him like a dark ocean and drowned him.

Toward dawn, he dreamt he had hidden himself in one of the naves of the Clementine Library. A librarian wearing dark glasses asked him: *What are you looking for?* Hladík answered: *God.* The Librarian told him: *God is in one of the letters on one of the pages of one of the 400,000 volumes of the Clementine. My fathers and the fathers of my fathers have sought after that letter. I've gone blind looking for it.* He removed his glasses, and Hladík saw that his eyes were dead. A reader came in to return an atlas. *This atlas is useless,* he said, and handed it to Hladík, who opened it at random. As if through a haze, he saw a map of India. With a sudden rush of assurance, he touched one of the tiniest letters. An ubiquitous voice said: *The time for your work has been granted.* Hladík awoke.

He remembered that the dreams of men belong to God, and that Maimonides wrote that the words of a dream are divine, when they are all separate and clear and are spoken by someone invisible. He dressed. Two soldiers entered his cell and ordered him to follow them.

From behind the door, Hladík had visualized a labyrinth of passageways, stairs, and connecting blocks. Reality was less rewarding: the party descended to an inner courtyard by a single iron stairway. Some soldiers—uniforms unbuttoned—were testing a motorcycle and disputing their conclusions. The sergeant looked at his watch: it was 8:44. They must wait until nine. Hladík, more insignificant than pitiful, sat down on a pile of firewood. He noticed that the soldiers' eyes avoided his. To make his wait easier, the sergeant offered him a cigarette. Hladík did not smoke. He accepted the cigarette out of politeness or humility. As he lit it, he saw that his hands shook. The day was clouding over. The soldiers spoke in low tones, as though he were already dead. Vainly, he strove to recall the woman of whom Julia de Weidenau was the symbol. . . .

The firing squad fell in and was brought to attention. Hladík, standing against the barracks wall, waited for the volley. Someone expressed fear the wall would be splashed with blood. The condemned man was ordered to step forward a few paces. Hladík recalled, absurdly, the preliminary maneuvers of a photographer. A heavy drop of rain grazed one of Hladík's temples and slowly rolled down his cheek. The sergeant barked the final command.

The physical universe stood still.

The rifles converged upon Hladík, but the men assigned to pull the triggers were immobile. The sergeant's arm eternalized an inconclusive gesture. Upon a courtyard flagstone a bee cast a stationary shadow. The wind had halted, as in a painted picture. Hladík began a shriek, a syllable, a twist of the hand. He realized he was paralyzed. Not a sound reached him from the stricken world.

He thought: *I'm in hell, I'm dead*.

He thought: *I've gone mad*.

He thought: *Time has come to a halt*.

Then he reflected that in that case, his thought, too, would have come to a halt. He was anxious to test this possibility: he repeated (without moving his lips) the mysterious Fourth Eclogue of Virgil. He imagined that the already remote soldiers shared his anxiety; he longed to communicate with them. He was astonished that he felt no fatigue, no vertigo from his protracted immobility. After an indeterminate length of time he fell asleep. On awakening he found the world still motionless and numb. The drop of water still clung to his cheek; the shadow of the bee still did not shift in the courtyard; the smoke from the cigarette he had thrown down did not blow away. Another "day" passed before Hladík understood.

He had asked God for an entire year in which to finish his work: His omnipotence had granted him the time. For his sake, God projected a secret miracle: German lead would kill him, at the determined hour, but in his mind a year would elapse between the command to fire and its execution. From perplexity he passed to stupor, from stupor to resignation, from resignation to sudden gratitude.

He disposed of no document but his own memory; the mastering of each hexameter as he added it, had imposed upon him a kind of fortunate discipline not imagined by those amateurs who forget their vague, ephemeral, paragraphs. He did not work for posterity, nor even for God, of whose literary preferences he possessed scant knowledge. Meticulous, unmoving, secretive, he wove his lofty invisible labyrinth in time. He worked the third act over twice. He eliminated some rather too-obvious symbols: the repeated striking of the hour, the music. There were no circumstances to constrain him. He omitted, condensed, amplified; occasionally, he chose the primitive version. He grew to love the courtyard, the barracks; one of the faces endlessly confronting him made him modify his conception of Roemerstadt's character. He discovered that the hard cacophonies which so distressed Flaubert are mere visual superstitions: debilities and annoyances of the written word, not of the sonorous, the sounding one. . . . He brought his drama to a conclusion: he lacked only a single epithet. He found it: the drop of water slid down his cheek. He began a wild cry, moved his face aside. A quadruple blast brought him down.

Jaromir Hladík died on March 29, at 9:02 in the morning.

—*Translated by* Anthony Kerrigan

CONJECTURAL POEM

Doctor Francisco Laprida, assassinated September 22, 1829, by the irregulars of Aldao, reflects before he dies:

The bullets whine on the last afternoon.
The wind is up, and full of ashes,
dispersing the day and the formless
war, and victory belongs to them,
to the barbarians: the gauchos have won.
And Francisco Narciso de Laprida, I,
who studied canon law and civil,
whose voice declared the independence
of these harsh provinces, am overthrown,
covered with blood and sweat,
without fear or hope, lost,
fleeing south through the farthest outskirts.
I'm like that captain in *Purgatorio*
fleeing afoot and leaving a trail of blood,
blinded and felled by death
where a dark river loses its name:
that's the way I'll fall. Today's the end.
The lateral night of the plains
lies in ambush to waylay me. I hear the hoofs
of my own hot death, searching me out,
I longed to be something else, a man of
sentiments, books, judgment,
and now will lie in a swamp under the open sky.
And yet, a secret joy inexplicably
exalts me. I've met my destiny,

my final South American destiny.
The manifold labyrinth my steps
wove through all these years since childhood
has brought me to this ruinous afternoon.
Now at this last point I find
the recondite code and cipher to my days,
the fate of Francisco de Laprida,
the missing letter, the perfect
form known to God from the start.
In the mirror of this night I find
the unexpected mien of my eternity.
The circle's closing. Thus may it be.
My feet are treading the shadows of pikes
pointed at me. The taunts of death,
the riders, the horses and their manes
are circling around me, hovering, the first
blow of the hard iron to rip at my chest,
the intimate knife at my throat . . .

—*Translated by* ANTHONY KERRIGAN

THE GIFTS

Let no one debase with pity or reprove
This declaration of God's mastery
Who with magnificent irony
Gave me at once books and the night.

Of this city of books he made two
Lightless eyes the owners, eyes that can
Read only in the library of dreams
Those senseless paragraphs that surrender

The dawns to their desire. In vain the day
Lavishes on them its infinite books,
Arduous as those arduous manuscripts
That were destroyed in Alexandria.

Of hunger and thirst (a Greek story has it)
A king dies amid fountains and gardens;
I drudge aimlessly about the limits
Of this enormous library of my blindness.

Encyclopedias, atlases, the East
And the West, centuries, dynasties,
Symbols, cosmos, and cosmogonies
Entice from the walls, but uselessly.

Within my darkness I slowly explore
The hollow half light with hesitant cane,
I who always imagined Paradise
To be a sort of library.

Something, which certainly is not named
By the word *chance*, governs these things;
Some other already received on other faded
Afternoons the many books and the dark.

Wandering through the heavy galleries,
I often feel with sacred vague horror
That I am that other, the dead one, who will
Have walked here too and on these very days.

Which of us is writing this poem
With plural I and a single darkness?
What difference the word that names me
If the curse is undivided and single?

Groussac or Borges, I look at this dear
World which collapses and goes out
In a pale indefinite ash
That resembles both the dream and oblivion.

—*Translated by* Irving Feldman

THE MOON

History tells us that in such time past
when so many real, imaginary
and doubtful things took place,
one man conceived the unwieldy

Plan of ciphering the universe
in one book and, infinitely rash,
built his high and mighty manuscript,
shaping and declaiming the final line.

But when about to praise his luck,
he lifted up his eyes, and saw
a burnished disk upon the air; startled,
he realized he'd left out the moon.

Though contrived, this little story
might well exemplify the mischief
that involves us all who take on
the job of turning real life into words.

Always the essential thing gets lost. That's
one rule holds true of every inspiration.
Nor will this résumé of my long
association with the moon escape it.

I don't know when I saw it first—
if in the sky prior to the doctrine
of the Greek, or in the evening darkening over
the patio with the fig tree and the well.

As they say, this unpredictable life
can be, among other things, quite beautiful.
That's how it was the evening we looked
at you, she and I—oh, shared moon!

Better than real nighttime moons, I can
recall the moons of poetry: the bewitched
dragon moon that thrills one in the ballad,
and, of course, Quevedo's bloody moon.

Then there was that other blood-red moon
John wrote of in his book of dreadful
prodigies and terrifying jubilees;
still other moons are clearer, silvery.

Pythagoras (according to one tradition)
used blood to write upon a mirror,
and men read it by reflection
in that other mirror called the moon.

There's an iron forest where a huge wolf
lives whose strange fate is
to knock the moon down and murder it
when the last dawn reddens the sea.

(This is well known in the prophetic North;
also, that on that day the ship made out
of all the fingernails of the dead will spread
a poison on the world's wide-open seas.)

When in Geneva or in Zurich once, luck
had it I too should become a poet,
it imposed on me, as on the rest, the secret
duty to define the moon.

By dint of scrupulous study,
I rang all the modest changes
under the lively apprehension that Lugones
might have used my *amber* or my *sand*.

As for exotic marble, smoke, cold snow—
these were for moons that lit up verses
never destined, in truth, to attain
the difficult distinction of typography.

I thought the poet such a man
as red Adam was in Paradise—
he gave everything its true,
precise, still unknown name.

Ariosto taught me that living in
the doubtful moon are all dreams,
the unattainable, lost time, all possibles
or impossibles (they're pretty much the same).

Apollodorus showed me the magic
shadow of triform Diana;
Hugo disclosed its golden sickle;
an Irishman his tragic moon of black.

So, while I was poking in this mine
of moons out of mythologies,
along it came, around the corner:
the celestial moon of every day.

Among the words, I know there's only
one for remembering or imagining it.
For me the secret is to use the word
humbly. And the word is—*moon*.

Now I don't dare stain its immaculate
appearance with one vain image.
I see it as indecipherable, daily
and apart from all my writing.

I know the moon, or the word *moon*,
is a character created for
the complex inditing of the rare
thing we all are, multiple and unique.

It's one of the symbols which fate
or chance gave man so that
one day in a glorious blaze, or agony,
he'd learn to write his own true name.

—*Translated by* Edwin Honig

THE ART OF POETRY

To gaze at a river made of time and water
and remember Time is another river.
To know we stray like a river
and our faces vanish like water.

To feel that waking is another dream
that dreams of not dreaming and that the death
we fear in our bones is the death
that every night we call a dream.

To see in every day and year a symbol
of all the days of man and his years,
and convert the outrage of the years
into a music, a sound and a symbol.

To see in death a dream, in the sunset
a golden sadness—such is poetry,
humble and immortal, poetry
returning, like dawn and sunset.

Sometimes at evening there's a face
that sees us from the deeps of a mirror.
Art must be that sort of mirror,
disclosing to each of us his face.

They say Ulysses, wearied of wonders,
wept with love on seeing Ithaca,
humble and green. Art is that Ithaca,
a green eternity, not wonders.

Art is endless like a river flowing,
passing, yet remaining, a mirror to the same
inconstant Heraclitus, who is the same
and yet another, like the river flowing.

—*Translated by* ANTHONY KERRIGAN

BORGES AND I

Things happen to him, the other one, to Borges. I stroll about Buenos Aires and stop, almost mechanically now perhaps, to look at the arch of an entranceway and the ironwork gate; news of Borges reaches me in the mail and I see his name on an academic ballot or in a biographical dictionary. I like hourglasses, maps, eighteenth-century typography, etymologies, the taste of coffee, and Robert Louis Stevenson's prose; he shares these preferences, but with a vanity that turns them into the attributes of an actor. It would be an exaggeration to say that our relationship is a hostile one; I live, I go on living, so that Borges may contrive his literature; and that literature justifies me. I do not find it hard to admit that he has achieved some valid pages, but these pages can not save me, perhaps because what is good no longer belongs to anyone, not even to him, the other one, but to the language or to tradition. In any case, I am destined to perish, definitively, and only some instant of me may live on in him. Little by little, I yield him ground, the whole terrain, though. I am quite aware of his perverse habit of magnifying and falsifying. Spinoza realized that all things strive to persist in their own nature: the stone eternally wishes to be stone and the tiger a tiger. I shall subsist in Borges, not in myself (assuming I am someone), and yet I recognize myself less in his books than in many another, or than in the intricate flourishes played on a guitar. Years ago I tried to free myself from him, and I went from the mythologies of the city suburbs to games with time and infinity, but now those games belong to Borges, and I will have to think up something else. Thus is my life a flight, and I lose everything, and everything belongs to oblivion, or to him.

I don't know which one of the two of us is writing this page.

—Translated by ANTHONY KERRIGAN

POEM WRITTEN IN A COPY OF BEOWULF

At various times, I have asked myself what reasons
moved me to study, while my night came down,
without particular hope of satisfaction,
the language of the blunt-tongued Anglo-Saxons.

Used up by the years, my memory
loses its grip on words that I have vainly
repeated and repeated. My life in the same way
weaves and unweaves its weary history.

Then I tell myself: it must be that the soul
has some secret, sufficient way of knowing
that it is immortal, that its vast, encompassing
circle can take in all, can accomplish all.

Beyond my anxiety, beyond this writing,
the universe waits, inexhaustible, inviting.

—*Translated by* ALASTAIR REID

EDITOR'S EPILOGUE

An exchange of letters between
Anthony Kerrigan and Alastair Reid

> Through the years, a man peoples a
> space with images of provinces, king-
> doms, mountains, bays, ships, islands,
> fishes, rooms, tools, stars, horses, and
> people. Shortly before his death, he
> discovers that the patient labyrinth
> of lines traces the image of his own
> face.
>
> —Borges

Dear Tony,

In these past few days, I have been working over the translations for the Borges book we agreed to do, and it has left me in a strange, indecisive state. Who wrote this book? I remember a conversation—I was sure it was with you, but now I am not sure of anything—in which we decided once to create a character and pool our energies to write books by him, thereby relieving ourselves of some of the responsibilities of being which books involve. Nadie puede escribir un libro, *as Borges reminds us. But I have the sudden feeling that this might be the book, for with these poems, I have kept coming across my own preoccupations, and writing English poems out of what is concealed in the Spanish. You, I imagine, have been doing much the same with the prose. Then I wonder, who is this Jorge Luis Borges? We have been working on these thin volumes of his for some years now, and have we ever met him, either of us? Other people say they have, but they may well be in the plot. We made him exist in English. We may have made him exist altogether—if he has any existence at all, that is, for he tells us all the time that he is dreaming himself, or being dreamt by somebody.*

And then the ripples run out from this doubtful center, and I wonder who you are. I know you well enough, on these odd, robust occasions when we meet; but it occurs to me now that you may be in league with Borges. You may be Borges, whoever he is. And then I arrive at the real, cruel center—who am I, anyway? Borges has involved me so utterly in his unbeing that I have translated some of myself out of existence. I am translated. The thing is, none of these translations can be in the least conclusive, not because of the language at all, but because of the insubstantial nature of the reality which the Spanish reflects waveringly, like an old, greening mirror, and which the English re-reflects, until nothing exists but reflection itself.

If, as Borges makes uncertainly clear to us, there are several Borgeses, whose existences are in doubt always, what can be said of his translators? For Borges is translating us, as we translate him; and we are adding extra selves, linguistic ones, to the already confused extensions of this man who has been playing with our existence for so long. Forgive me if I stop short; any more speculation might prove dangerous. I have a mind now to translate Borges' English poems into Spanish, to see if I can win back any lost ground. I send this to you, with no confidence that it will ever reach you, whoever you are.

Alastair

Dear Alastair,

I know well enough who you *are: I saw you last on my left side in the little patio of* La Juncosa, *off the Plaza de San Joaquín, in Barcelona. It was the time of the* rovellons, *that glory among Catalan mushrooms, and there was a parochial feast just outside the restaurant. You reacted to both events: by ordering the former and ignoring the latter. Yes, yes, you existed that night, and those* rovellons *continue being unique. Nothing has changed about that trivial but immortal meal: that table will always be set. (And, yes, you spoke of your recent visit to Cuba, where you had not been allowed to make the visit. They had you down as a libertarian, and three libertarians had just been shot in Camagüey. You pretended not to speak Spanish, and looked at a girl's rump in militiaman's pants while they talked.) I also know who you are because the first time I saw you striding against the Mallorcan horizon at Deyá the friend with you had no right arm.*

As proof of my own identity I won't adduce my FBI file, which lists me as an Ohlerite-Trotskyite member of the Socialist Party in Los Angeles (permanent), though I was in fact a conservator of legends, or reactionary anarchist, by late adolescence. I will only mention that lately in Dublin I recognized the tune an Irish fiddler was playing in a pub as one my father, an Irish fiddler, had played in Cuba, the same Cuba where you were not allowed to be, a tune I thought he thought he had composed himself.

As for Borges, I need merely recall to you the sound of keening at the rumors of his death in November of 1957.

In Paris Gallimard solemnly determined to issue his work, as news of the transcendental event pulsated like a swollen vein in the literary press (though the publishers had never heard of his existence until his death was postulated as a possibility). In Palma de Mallorca, a little pamphlet in memoriam was issued. ("En homenaje a Jorge Luis Borges, muerto en noviembre de 1957.") *Subsequently, when the news of his death died away, chroniclers spoke of his blindness, and related it to his directing the accumulation of (unseen) books in the National Library in Buenos Aires, and to his attending (unseeable) sound films while on a visit to New Mexico. I myself (I assume you do, now, recognize the poignancy—past and future: both nostalgic and prescient—of the* rovellons *and the lack of an arm: tangible suggestions of my existence, tangential to yours) wrote about a meeting with him in Madrid, though in actual fact, as they say very often in Dublin, stressing concreteness with a certain uncertainty, I did not get to Madrid at that time. But the daily* ABC, *the opaque and honest monarchist organ in the capital, recorded daily items about his four-day stay. So that unless my edition of the* ABC *was a unique copy, differing from the thousands of other* ABC's *for those days, and included an entry which others did not, Borges was in Madrid in 1963. And I might have met him, had my own report of the meeting—published in Paris in French, assembled according to the largely immutable laws of that deathless language—taken another form.*

I ask you, then, how can a man perturb the pages of Paris literary journals with his death if he has never really lived? And how could a monarchist daily in Madrid mistake his visit to that city? There are circumstances and circumstances, too many for one chronicler to control, but I cling to the concrete notion of Borges not dying in 1957, and to the possibility of one's having been able to meet him in Madrid in 1963, just as I wrote.

I can give evidence, too, on the other translators of this collective "Borges," of course. They have all signed their names in many places and, unless Borges wrote all their books and poems—which, though he could no doubt do in imitation of them, he doubtless did not do it before they did so themselves: that is, write all their own words precisely in imitation of themselves before anyone else might attempt to do so—if Borges did not write their books, then, and all the translations of them, they are, our fellow translators, still at their task of self-identification, in firsthand and primary mime. (To think that Borges would have cared to translate the original work of our fellow translators into other tongues is to be excessive. No, our fellow translators' translations vouch for them, and for us.) I know people who between them know all of them, but in different ways than I do. In the end, all identification comes down to trifles, and never to the fireproof files: the drunken sound of a "translator's" voice on a certain night, the rain lashing a two-way pattern on his raincoat, his accent in a foreign tongue, a look avoided.

Borges, I feel, would not necessarily be loath to accept us, intrinsically and extrinsically, as collaborators in his existence, collaborators in existing him. Any one of us, or all of us in composite form, are capable of liking "hourglasses, maps, eighteenth-century typography, etymologies, the taste of coffee, and Robert Louis Stevenson's prose" just like the Borges who is not "Borges" but himself, not Borges-Borges, but I-Borges; albeit as Northerners (though not inevitably more Anglo-Saxon than Borges) and amateur Hispanists by avocation, we would, most of us, be more prone to reading the prose of Valle-Inclán, the one-armed Carlist, or Pío Baroja, the Madrid Basque, at this stage in our history, than that of Stevenson.

In sum: if I exist (and there is even evidence beyond the sound in my ears of my father's tune still haunting the

Dublin air), so do you (and there is more than the rovellons *to vouch for it). And if we do, so does Borges (and there is further evidence than his not having died in 1957 or than the Madrid visit documented in the honest monarchist* ABC *and my report of our not having met written for the French journal* L'Herne). *So that Borges, here, in this book, collaborates in existing us, just as we here exist him. He is our testimonial, and we his. Do we need any further voucher for today, for tonight, the eve of the feast of* Nuestra Señora de la O, *Our Lady of the O?*

Yours in faith,

Tony